# SPACE FRONTIERS

## Living and Working in Space

Helen Whittaker

MACMILLAN LIBRARY

First published in 2010 by
MACMILLAN EDUCATION AUSTRALIA PTY LTD
15–19 Claremont Street, South Yarra 3141

Visit our website at www.macmillan.com.au or go directly to www.macmillanlibrary.com.au

Associated companies and representatives throughout the world.



National Library of Australia Cataloguing-in-Publication entry

Whittaker, Helen.
Living and Working in Space / Helen Whittaker
ISBN: 978 1 4202 7333 5 (hbk.)
Series: Whittaker, Helen. Space Frontiers.
Includes index.
Target Audience: For primary school age.
Subjects: Astronauts—Juvenile literature. Manned space flight—Juvenile literature.
Outer space—Juvenile literature.
629.45

Edited by Laura Jeanne Gobal
Text and cover design by Cristina Neri, Canary Graphic Design
Page layout by Cristina Neri, Canary Graphic Design
Photo research by Brendan and Debbie Gallagher
Illustrations by Alan Laver

Printed in China

**Acknowledgements**
The author and the publisher are grateful to the following for permission to reproduce copyright material:

Front cover photos of Flight Engineer Sunita L. Williams on an EVA on the *International Space Station*, courtesy of NASA/HSF; blue nebula background © sololos/iStockphoto.

Photographs courtesy of:
NASA/HSF, **3** (both), **5**, **9**, **10**, **12**, **13** (both), **14**, **15**, **16**, **17**, **18**, **19** (top), **20**, **21**, **22**, **23**, **25**, **28**, **29**, **30**, back cover; ASA/JPL-Caltech/Potsdam Univ, **6–7**; NASA/JSC, Eugene Cernan, **4**; NASA/MSFC, **24**, **26**, **27**; NASA/MSFC, Terry Leibold, **11**; Photolibrary/Science Photo Library, **8**.

Images used in design and background on each page © prokhorov/iStockphoto, Soubrette/iStockphoto.

While every care has been taken to trace and acknowledge copyright, the publisher tenders their apologies for any accidental infringement where copyright has proved untraceable. Where the attempt has been unsuccessful, the publisher welcomes information that would redress the situation.

# CONTENTS

## Glossary words

When a word is printed in **bold**, you can look up its meaning in the Glossary on page 31.

# SPACE FRONTIERS

*A frontier is an area that is only just starting to be discovered. Humans have now explored almost the whole planet, so there are very few frontiers left on Earth. However, there is another frontier for us to explore and it is bigger than we can possibly imagine – space.*

**Spaceflight is one way of exploring the frontier of space. Astronaut Harrison Schmitt collects Moon rocks during the Apollo 17 mission in December 1972.**

## Where is space?

Space begins where Earth's **atmosphere** ends. The atmosphere thins out gradually, so there is no clear boundary marking where space begins. However, most scientists define space as beginning at an altitude of 100 kilometres (62 miles). Space extends to the very edge of the universe. Scientists do not know where the universe ends, so no one knows how big space is.

## Exploring space

Humans began exploring space just by looking at the night sky. The invention of the telescope in the 1600s and improvements in its design have allowed us to see more of the universe. Since the 1950s, there has been another way to explore space – spaceflight. Through spaceflight, humans have **orbited** Earth, visited the Moon and sent space probes, or small unmanned spacecraft, to explore our **solar system**.

# LIVING AND WORKING IN SPACE

*Manned spaceflights are an important part of space exploration. Crews on space shuttle flights, which are operated by the National Aeronautics and Space Administration (NASA), spend about two weeks in space. Crews on the International Space Station (ISS) spend up to six months living and working in space.*

## Why send people to live and work in space?

Although machines are becoming more and more sophisticated, there are still many jobs in space that only a human can do. One of the purposes of sending people to live and work in space is to study the effects of long periods of spaceflight on the human body, in preparation for future manned flights to Mars and beyond.

## The challenges of living and working in space

**Microgravity**, which astronauts experience during a spaceflight, makes many tasks more difficult than they would be on Earth. It also affects the astronauts' bodies, causing muscles to waste away and bones to lose density. Some of the other challenges of living and working in space are cramped conditions, feeling alone and a limited supply of water and other essentials.

### Animals and plants in space

Humans are not the only living things to experience space. Spiders, ants, bees and fish are also sent into space so scientists can find out how microgravity affects them. Plants are grown in space, too. When humans eventually make the long journey to Mars, they will need to be able to grow food on their spacecraft.

**Astronauts carry out important research in space to help us understand more about the universe and also improve life on Earth.**

# A TIMELINE OF LIVING AND WORKING IN SPACE

*The timeline below shows every space program that has sent human beings into space.*

1960 1965 1970 1975 1980

**Vostok** 1961–1963
**Description:** The **Soviet Union**'s first manned spaceflight program
**Flights:** Six of 11 flights carried humans. Four earlier flights carried animals, including dogs, mice, rats and a guinea pig.
**Achievements:** Yuri Gagarin became the first man in space in April 1961 on Vostok 1. Valentina Tereshkova became the first woman in space in June 1963 on Vostok 6.

**Project Mercury** 1959–1963
**Description:** The United States's first manned spaceflight program
**Flights:** Out of 26 flights, only the final 6 carried astronauts. Four of the test flights carried animals.
**Achievements:** American astronaut Alan Shepard became the second person in space in May 1961, flying *Freedom 7*.

**Voskhod** 1964–1965
**Description:** A short-lived program that made important advances in manned spaceflight
**Flights:** There were one unmanned and two manned flights.
**Achievements:** Voskhod 1, launched in October 1964, was the first spaceflight to carry more than one person. It had a crew of three. Alexei Leonov made the world's first ever spacewalk in March 1965 on Voskhod 2.

**Project Gemini** 1965–1966
**Description:** Developed technology needed to send humans to the Moon
**Flights:** Ten of 12 flights were manned.
**Achievements:** In March 1966, *Gemini 8* became the first spacecraft to **dock** with another spacecraft in space.

**Apollo Program** 1963–1972
**Description:** The only program to date that has sent humans to the Moon
**Flights:** There were 6 unmanned test flights and 11 manned missions, of which 6 landed on the Moon.
**Achievements:** Apollo 11 astronauts Neil Armstrong and Edwin 'Buzz' Aldrin became the first human beings to walk on the Moon in July 1969.

**Soyuz** 1966–present
**Description:** Originally intended to send humans to the Moon, but since 1971, it has transported crews to and from space stations
**Flights:** There have been 26 unmanned test flights and 101 manned flights to date.
**Achievements:** Soyuz is the longest-running manned spaceflight program.

**Space Transportation System (space shuttle)** 1972–2010
**Description:** A reusable spacecraft designed for use in low Earth **orbit**
**Flights:** There were many suborbital test flights, some manned, others nc and to date, 132 manned orbital flights have been completed.
**Achievements:** The space shuttle was the first reusable spacecraft and th first to land like an aeroplane.

**Salyut** 1971–1982
**Description:** A series of Soviet space stations
**Achievements:** *Salyut 1*, launched in April 1971, was the world's first space station.

***Skylab*** 1973–1979
**Description:** The United States's first space station
**Achievements:** *Skylab* was only occupied for 171 days, but visiting astronauts spent about 2000 hours conducting medical and scientific experiments.

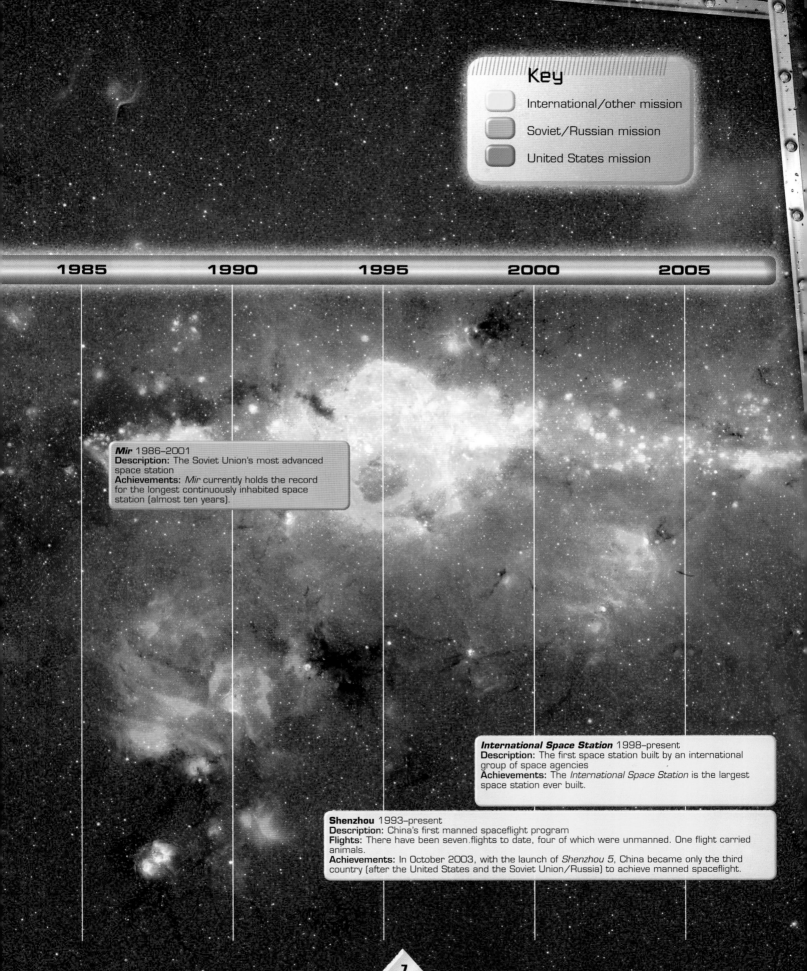

**Key**

International/other mission

Soviet/Russian mission

United States mission

**1985** | **1990** | **1995** | **2000** | **2005**

***Mir*** 1986–2001
**Description:** The Soviet Union's most advanced space station
**Achievements:** *Mir* currently holds the record for the longest continuously inhabited space station (almost ten years).

***International Space Station*** 1998–present
**Description:** The first space station built by an international group of space agencies
**Achievements:** The *International Space Station* is the largest space station ever built.

**Shenzhou** 1993–present
**Description:** China's first manned spaceflight program
**Flights:** There have been seven flights to date, four of which were unmanned. One flight carried animals.
**Achievements:** In October 2003, with the launch of *Shenzhou 5*, China became only the third country (after the United States and the Soviet Union/Russia) to achieve manned spaceflight.

# LIVING AND WORKING IN SPACE – THEN AND NOW

*Not long after the first manned spaceflight in 1961, which lasted less than two hours, humans were living in space for days and even weeks at a time. These days, crews on the International Space Station spend up to six months living and working in space.*

## The first humans in space

By 1962, astronauts from the **Soviet Union** were spending several days in **orbit** and, by 1965, American astronauts were spending up to two weeks at a time in space. One problem on these early spaceflights was space sickness. Back then, missions had no more than three crewmembers, so one person falling ill for a few days would disrupt the entire mission.

### Space sickness

About half of all space travellers suffer space sickness, or Space Adaptation Syndrome, to some degree. Symptoms of space sickness include dizziness, headaches, **nausea** and vomiting. Fortunately, the effects usually last only two or three days.

**Russian astronaut Valentina Tereshkova was the first woman in space. Her flight on board Vostok 6 was launched on 16 June 1963. She spent almost three days in orbit.**

This photograph of the *Mir* space station was taken from the space shuttle *Discovery* in June 1998.

## The first space stations

The world's first space station was the Soviet Union's *Salyut 1*, launched in 1971. The United States's first space station was *Skylab*, launched in 1973. Early space stations were made up of a single module and conditions on board were very cramped. The first multi-module space station was the Soviet Union's *Mir*, which was constructed in space between 1986 and 1996.

## *The* International Space Station

Sixteen countries are working together to complete the *International Space Station*, which is the only space station currently in operation. Its main purpose is to carry out scientific research. The *ISS* is made up of 15 separate modules, including laboratories, **docking** compartments, **airlocks** and living quarters.

The table below shows how far space stations have come since the days of *Salyut 1*. As the number of modules increased, so did the living and working areas, shown below as living volume. More astronauts can be sent on missions to the *ISS* now to conduct construction work, repairs and experiments.

| Space station | *Salyut 1* | *Skylab* | *Mir* | *ISS* |
|---|---|---|---|---|
| **Number of modules** | 1 | 1 | 7 | 15 |
| **Weight (in kilograms/pounds)** | 18 425 kg (40 620 lb) | 90 605 kg (199 750 lb) | 124 340 kg (274 123 lb) | 303 663 kg (669 462 lb) |
| **Living volume (in cubic metres/cubic feet)** | 99 $m^3$ (3500 $ft^3$) | 360 $m^3$ (12 700 $ft^3$) | 350 $m^3$ (12 360 $ft^3$) | 358 $m^3$ (12 643 $ft^3$) |
| **Crew** | 3 | 3 | 3 | 6 |

# TRAINING TO LIVE AND WORK IN SPACE

*Astronauts train for a very long time. They must know their spacecraft completely and know what to do in an emergency. They also need to practise moving and working in a spacesuit.*

## Getting to know the spacecraft

During training, astronauts spend hundreds of hours in simulators. A simulator is a full-size model of a spacecraft. Astronauts learn how to operate all the spacecraft's systems and practise dealing with emergencies while in the simulator. Simulations can also take the form of **virtual reality** computer programs, which astronauts interact with using special headsets and gloves.

**American astronaut Joseph Acaba trains with a virtual reality program at Johnson Space Centre in the United States before his mission on the space shuttle *Discovery* in 2009.**

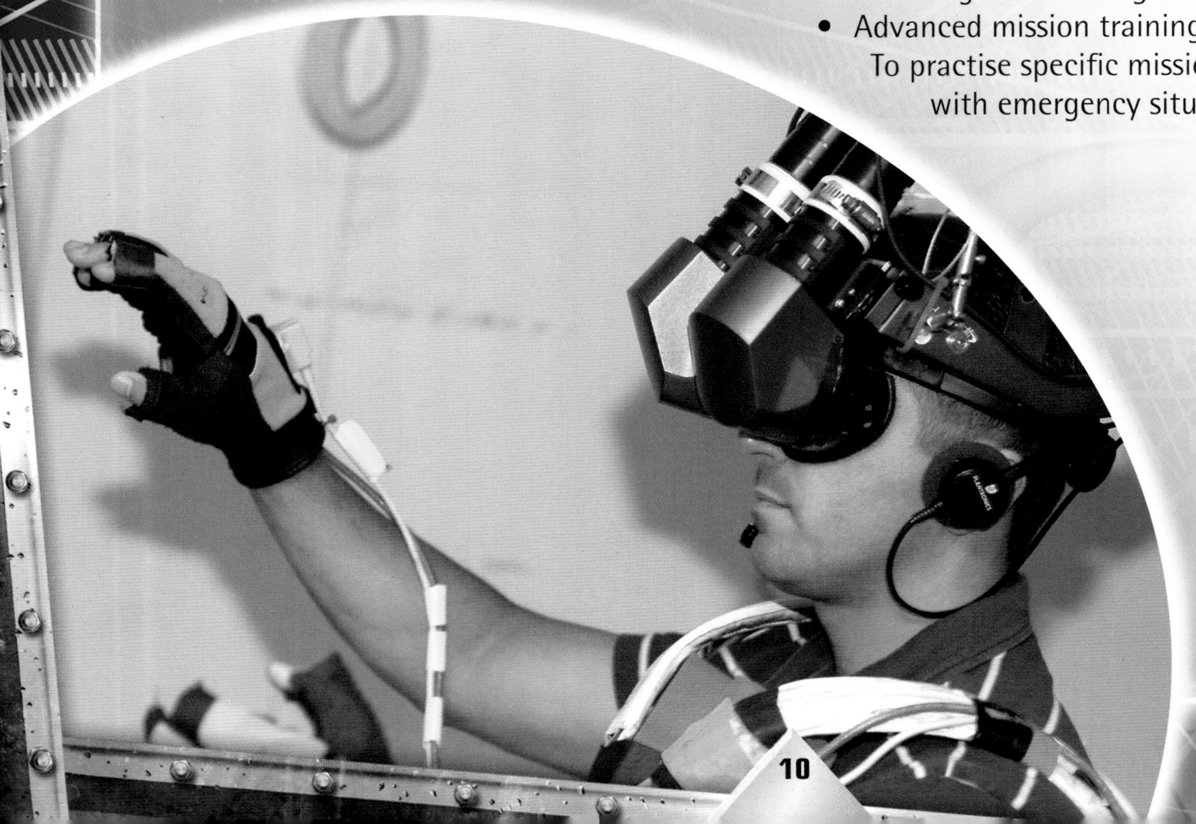

## The five areas of astronaut training

Astronauts undergo training in five important areas.

- Classroom work
  To study **aerodynamics**, physics, human biology and computer science
- Flight training
  To learn to fly an aeroplane
- Survival training
  To learn how to survive after an unplanned landing in water or on land
- Basic mission training
  To get to know the spacecraft and prepare for living and working in **microgravity**
- Advanced mission training
  To practise specific mission tasks and deal with emergency situations

**Astronauts train underwater at Marshall Space Flight Centre in the United States to test parts for the *International Space Station*. Divers are in the water to offer help if astronauts need it.**

## The Vomit Comet

The Vomit Comet refers to any aircraft that is used to provide a weightless environment. It does this by following a **parabolic** flight path, which leaves its occupants in a state of **free fall** for about 25 seconds out of every 65. This process generally makes most of its occupants experience **nausea**.

## *Training for weightlessness*

To be able to live and work in space, astronauts need to do more than just learn new skills. They also need to prepare for microgravity. This means they have to relearn how to do the simple things they do every day, but while weightless. To do so, they experience weightlessness in an aeroplane nicknamed the Vomit Comet. They also learn to scuba dive.

## *Training for spacewalks*

To practise moving around and working in microgravity while wearing a spacesuit, astronauts train in a large swimming pool. Their spacesuits are weighted to give them **neutral buoyancy** in the water. This simulates the feeling of weightlessness. While underwater, the astronauts practise the tasks they will perform while working outside the spacecraft.

# FOOD IN SPACE

*Organising the food for any expedition is a challenge. Due to the unique conditions in space, organising the food for a space mission is even more challenging.*

## Difficulties with food in space

Cooking food in space is almost impossible – weightless eggs and weightless bacon will not stay in the frying pan! Instead, astronauts reheat precooked food and rehydrate dried food by adding hot water. It is important to avoid foods that crumble because crumbs might float away and get stuck inside equipment. For this reason, salt, pepper and other condiments are in liquid form.

**American astronauts Shane Kimbrough and Sandra Magnus attempt to catch their fruit on board the space shuttle *Endeavour*.**

## Types of space food

The table below shows the main types of food eaten in space.

| Food category | Explanation | Examples |
| --- | --- | --- |
| fresh | food that is not processed in any way | apples and bananas |
| frozen | quick-frozen to prevent ice crystals from forming and to preserve taste | quiches, casseroles and chicken pot pie |
| intermediate moisture | partially dried food | dried peaches, dried apricots and beef jerky |
| irradiated | cooked and packed in foil pouches, and **sterilised** using **ionising radiation** | beef steak and roast turkey |
| natural form | untreated food sealed in foil pouches | biscuits, nuts and muesli bars |
| rehydratable | dried food that can be prepared by adding hot water | porridge |
| thermostabilised | heat-treated and sealed in cans or pots | tuna, lamb with vegetables and puddings |

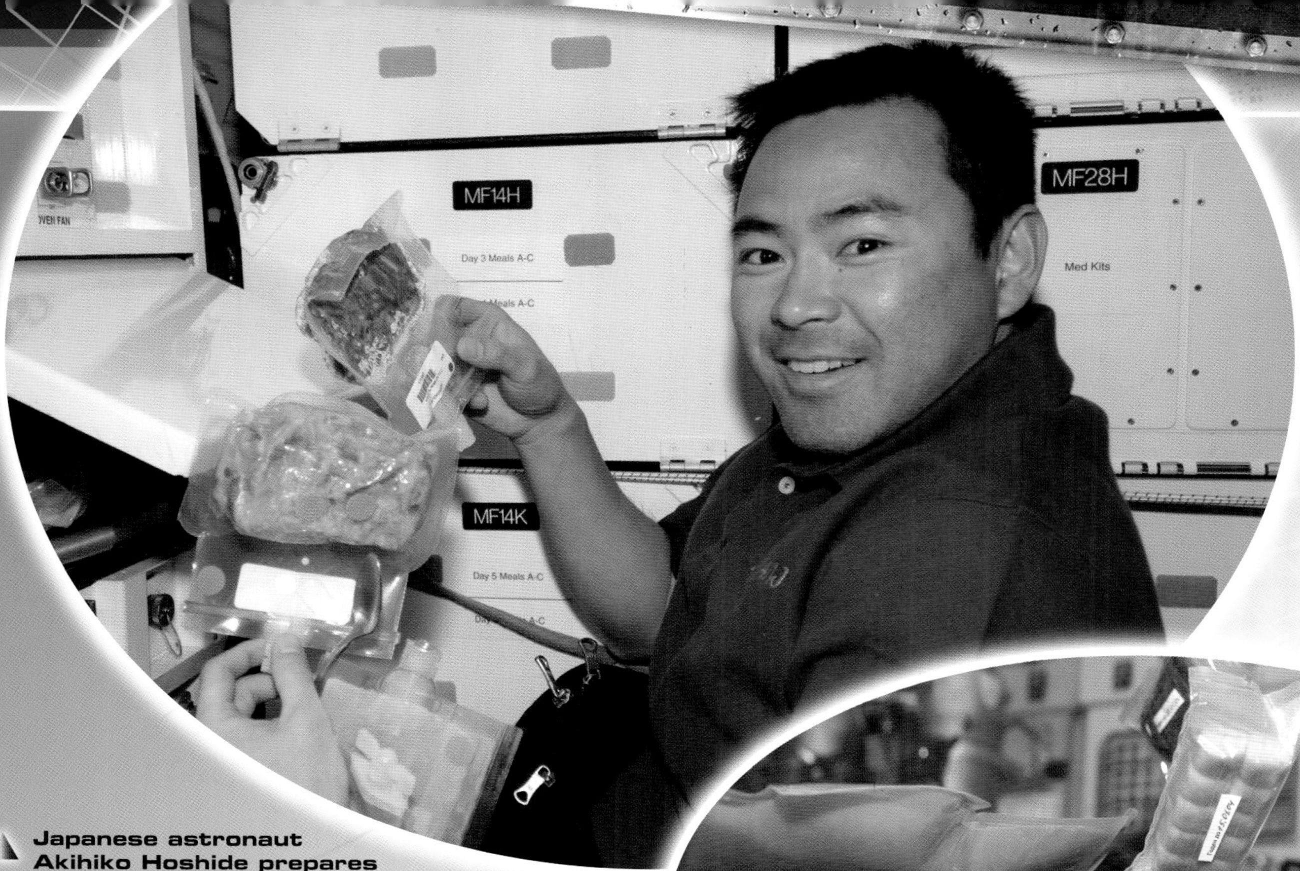

Japanese astronaut Akihiko Hoshide prepares to have a meal on the space shuttle *Discovery*.

Food is stored in different packaging as it has to be prepared in different ways.

## Meals in space

Some space foods can be eaten just as they are, but others need to be heated in a food warmer. Drinks and rehydratable food are prepared by adding water and mixing. Astronauts use a meal tray with Velcro strips to hold their food in place. After the meal, they clean their trays and eating utensils with wet wipes.

### Did you know?

On the *International Space Station*, crewmembers do not sit down to eat. Instead, they simply float next to the table.

## Space menus

Here is a typical dinner menu on the *International Space Station*.

| Menu item | Type of food |
|---|---|
| prawn cocktail | rehydratable |
| beef steak | irradiated |
| macaroni and cheese | rehydratable |
| fruit cocktail | thermostabilised |
| strawberry drink | beverage |
| tea with lemon | beverage |

# HOUSEWORK IN SPACE

*Just like people on Earth, astronauts have household chores. In fact, it is even more important that they stay on top of these chores because their lives may depend on it.*

## Cleaning

The crew of the *International Space Station* follows a strict cleaning schedule to keep **microorganisms**, such as viruses, bacteria and fungi, at bay. Microorganisms can affect the health of the crew and can 'eat' their way through the hard surfaces of a spacecraft.

**American astronaut Sunita Williams collects a sample of air in the Destiny laboratory of the *International Space Station*. This is part of the procedure known as SWAB (Surface, Water and Air Biocharacterisation).**

### SWAB (Surface, Water and Air Biocharacterisation)

SWAB is an ongoing procedure on the *International Space Station*. It examines air, surface and water samples for microorganisms and **allergens**. In the short term, it alerts the crew to any potential problems so they can take action. In the long term, it will contribute to the development of healthier spacecraft environments.

## Did you know?

One of the exterior checks that space shuttle astronauts carry out during spacewalks involves taking photographs of the heat shield using an **infrared camera**. This camera helps them detect damage much more effectively than a conventional camera.

**American astronaut Michael Barratt performs in-flight maintenance in the Zvezda Service Module of the *International Space Station*.**

## *Taking out the rubbish*

Astronauts on short spaceflights bring all their rubbish back to Earth for recycling and disposal. On the *ISS*, crewmembers load waste containers onto a supply vehicle **docked** at the station. When this vehicle is full, it undocks from the *ISS* and re-enters Earth's **atmosphere**, burning up as it does so.

## *Home maintenance*

To keep the spacecraft running safely, astronauts perform daily checks of all the spacecraft's systems, including power, navigation, computers and life-support. Then they repair or replace parts as required. They also put on their spacesuits and inspect the outside of the spacecraft to check for damage sustained during launch or caused by **micrometeoroid** impacts during **orbit**.

# HYGIENE IN SPACE

*Personal hygiene is very important in space. Astronauts work in a confined environment in close contact with each other, so infection can spread quickly. An astronaut who falls sick cannot visit a doctor or go to a hospital.*

## Washing

Each astronaut has his or her own personal hygiene kit. Astronauts can shave and brush their teeth normally, but there are no showers in space. They have to take sponge baths and wash their hair with rinse-free shampoo. The bathroom on board the *International Space Station* is called the hygiene centre.

**American astronaut James Voss shaves with an electric razor in the Zvezda Service Module of the *International Space Station*.**

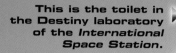

This is the toilet in the Destiny laboratory of the *International Space Station*.

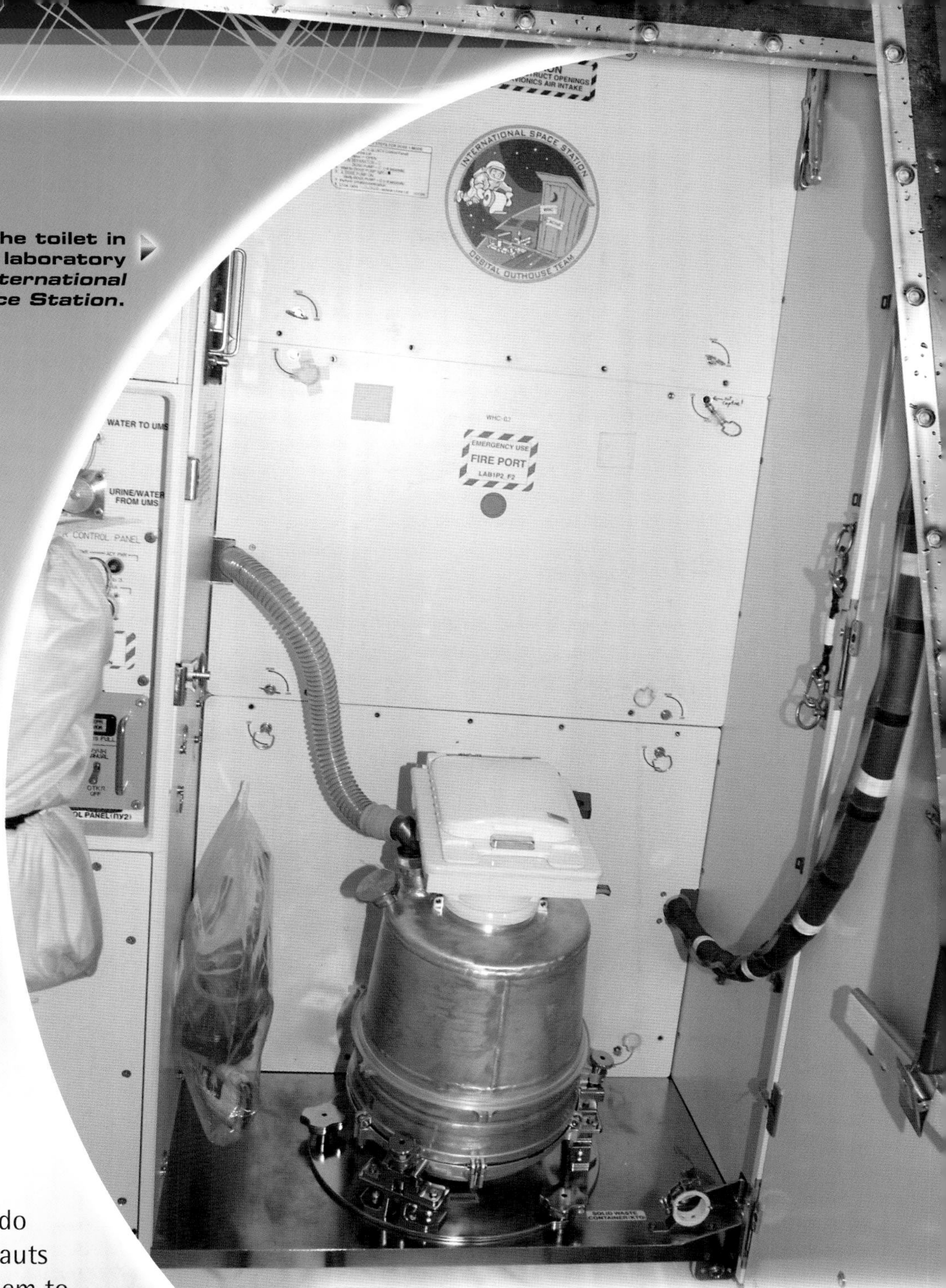


## Going to the toilet

An ordinary toilet relies on **gravity** and would not work in space. Astronauts use a special space toilet. Each astronaut has their own personal urine funnel. When they want to sit on the toilet, they have to strap themselves down. The toilet works like a vacuum cleaner, sucking air and waste into the waste tank.

## Doing the laundry

Space is not a good place to do laundry. Space shuttle astronauts bring enough clothes with them to last the entire mission and they take their dirty laundry back home. On the *ISS*, clean clothes are provided by a supply vehicle and dirty clothes are placed in the vehicle to be burned.

### Water on the *International Space Station*

Water is in limited supply on the *ISS*. All of the station's wastewater, including the crew's urine, is sent to an on-board water treatment plant, where it is thoroughly cleaned. It is then used again.

# Clothing in Space

*Astronauts wear different types of clothing at different times. During launch and **re-entry** they wear a pressure suit. Once in space, they wear everyday clothes. When working outside the spacecraft they wear a spacesuit.*

## Pressure suits

Astronauts wear a pressure suit during launch and re-entry to give them a better chance of surviving if they have to eject from the spacecraft. The pressure suit includes oxygen tanks, a parachute, a life raft, a radio, **flares** and enough drinking water for a day. The entire suit weighs about 35 kg (80 lb).

**American astronaut Charles Hobaugh is helped into a pressure suit during a water survival training session at Johnson Space Centre.**

## Putting on a pressure suit

Space shuttle astronauts spend up to 45 minutes getting into their pressure suits and testing the different parts to ensure they work.

**STEP 1:** In private, each astronaut puts on a thermal undersuit.

**STEP 2:** Technicians help the astronaut put on the pressure suit. Legs go in first, followed by arms.

**STEP 3:** Next, the astronaut pushes his or her head through the metal neck ring. It is a bit of a squeeze getting the astronaut's head into the suit because there is a tight seal around the neck.

**STEP 4:** Technicians zip up the suit and help the astronaut into the special boots.

**STEP 5:** The helmet and gloves are put on and locked in place with metal rings. The suit is checked for airtightness, then the helmet and gloves are removed until the astronaut is seated in the spacecraft.

**STEP 6:** Each astronaut's pockets are packed with survival items such as flares and a radio.

**STEP 7:** The crew then travels by van to the launch pad. In the van, they can plug into a cooling unit to stop themselves from overheating in the heavy suits.

**STEP 8:** At the launch pad, astronauts put on their parachutes and communications headsets.

**STEP 9:** While the astronauts are being strapped into their seats on the spacecraft, technicians help them put on their gloves and helmets to prepare for launch.

American astronauts Steven Swanson (right) and Richard Arnold (left) are helped into their spacesuits, or Extravehicular Mobility Units (EMUs).

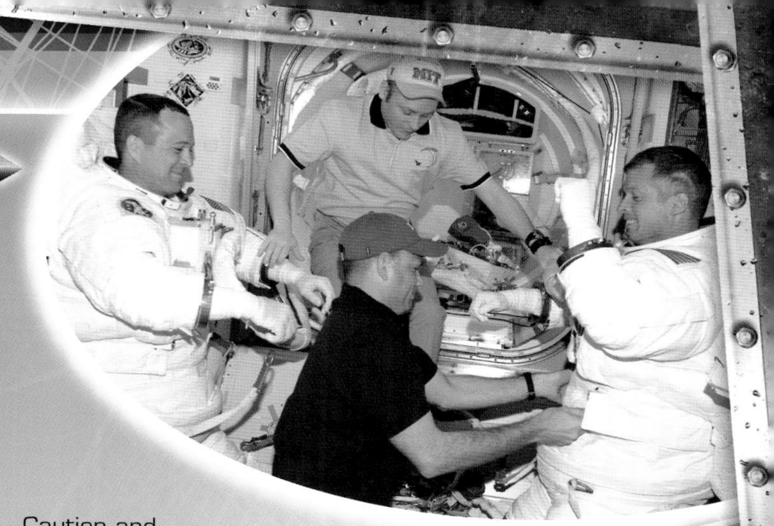

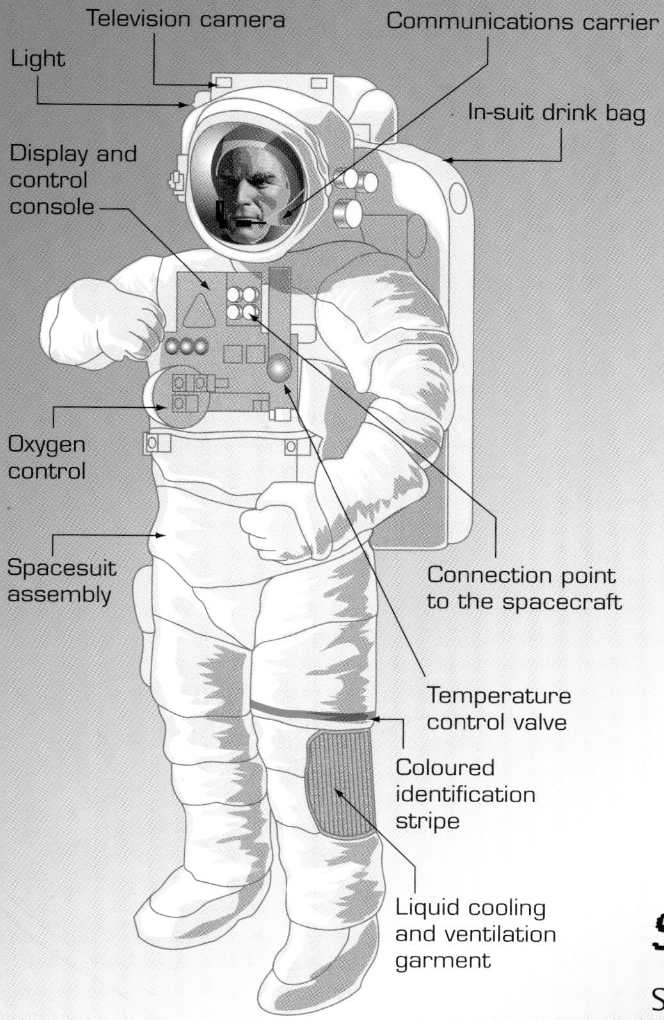


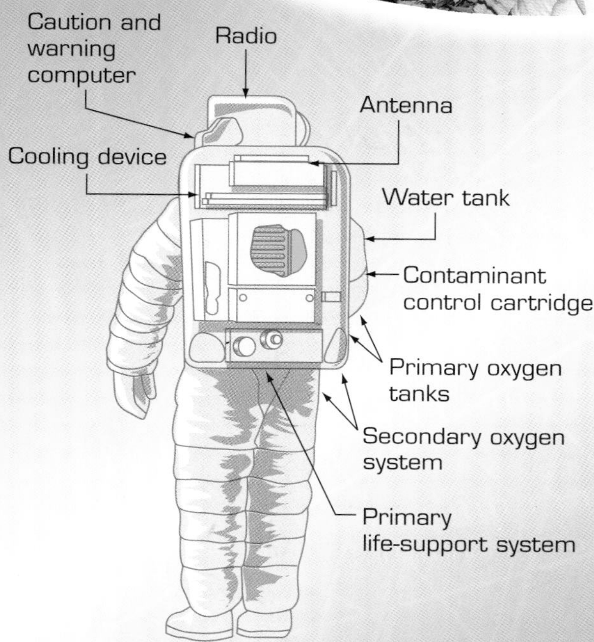


This illustration shows the EMU used by NASA astronauts during spacewalks.

## Spacesuits

Spacesuits are worn whenever an astronaut works outside the spacecraft. Without a spacesuit, astronauts would be unable to breathe in the vacuum of space and their bodies would start reacting to the lack of pressure outside Earth's **atmosphere**.

The spacesuit includes underwear with a network of tubes attached. Water flows through the tubes to keep the astronaut's body cool. The main suit, with pants, boots, upper body, sleeves, gloves and helmet, protects the astronaut from the environment. A backpack houses the life-support system, which can be managed by a control pack on the front of the suit.

## Everyday clothes

Most of the time, astronauts wear everyday clothes such as T-shirts, shorts, pants and jumpers. On the *International Space Station*, astronauts are not allowed to change their clothes as often as they would on Earth. They change their underwear and socks every other day and have fresh exercise clothes every three days. Their work clothes have to last for ten days.

# Sleeping in Space

*Astronauts need sleep just like anyone else, but without the force of gravity, lying down to sleep is difficult! The way astronauts sleep in space is very different to the way we sleep on Earth.*

## Challenges of sleeping in space

In **orbit**, sleeping astronauts would float around and bump into things unless they were strapped in. However, even when strapped in, astronauts do not feel like they are lying down, so some of them have trouble falling asleep.

**Italian astronaut Paolo Nespoli (right) and American crewmembers Pamela Melroy (left) and George Zamka (centre) take a nap on the space shuttle *Discovery*.**

## *Sleeping on the space shuttle*

With up to seven crewmembers on the space shuttle at any time and not much room to spare, sleeping conditions can be cramped. Astronauts can sleep in their seats or in a sleeping bag strapped to the wall. They are woken every morning by a different tune broadcast by Mission Control in Texas, the United States.

## *Sleeping on the* International Space Station

Each crewmember on the *ISS* has their own cabin, which is about the size of a telephone booth. The cabin has a laptop computer, storage for personal belongings and a sleeping bag strapped to the wall. Some cabins have a window with a blind. In the morning, crewmembers are woken by an alarm clock.

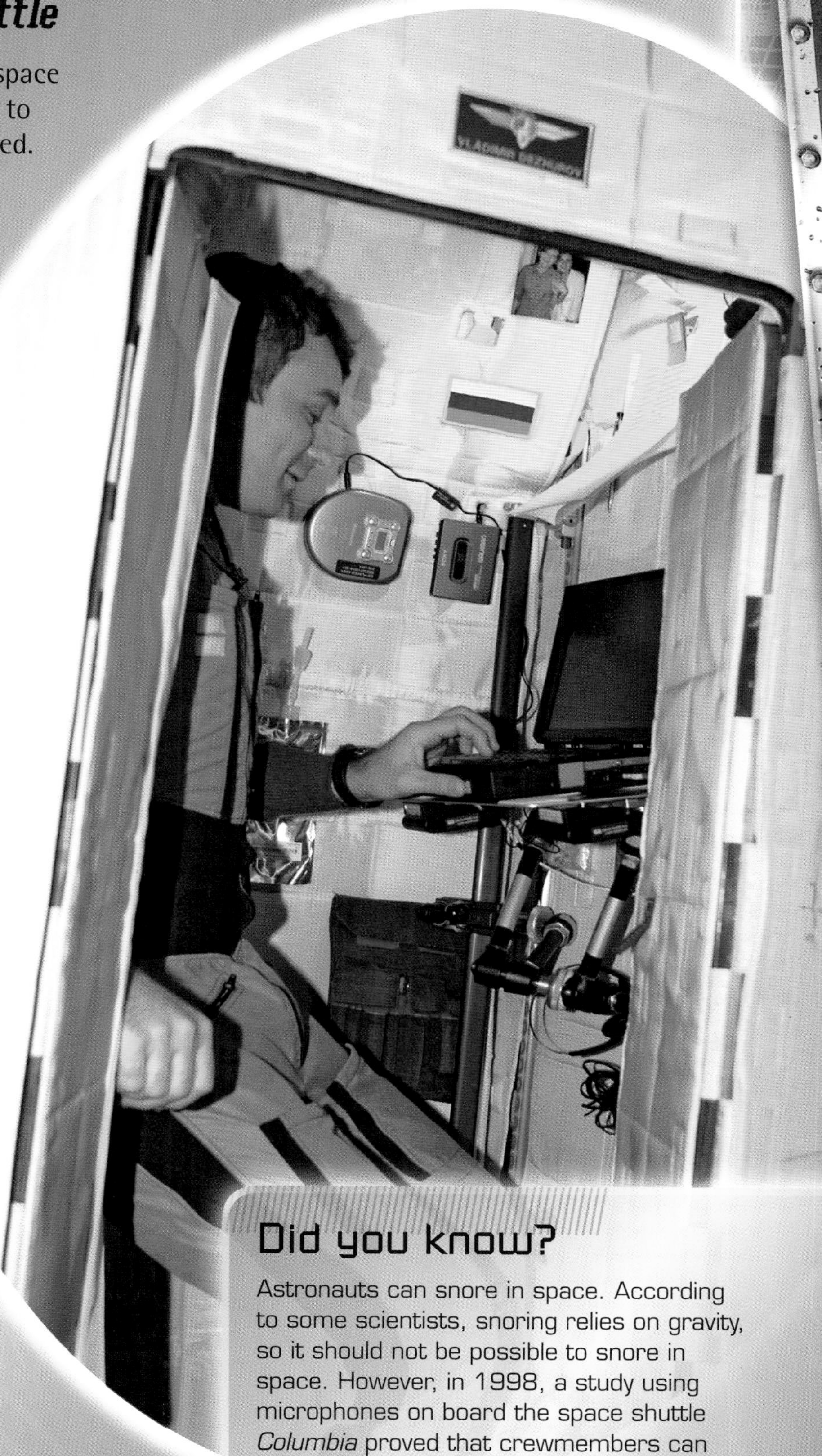

**Russian astronaut Vladimir Dezhurov works on a laptop computer in his cabin on the *International Space Station.* The laptop and other equipment are attached to the wall to prevent them from floating away.**

### Did you know?

Astronauts can snore in space. According to some scientists, snoring relies on gravity, so it should not be possible to snore in space. However, in 1998, a study using microphones on board the space shuttle *Columbia* proved that crewmembers can and do snore while in orbit.

# Staying Healthy in Space

*The human body evolved over time to cope with Earth's **gravity**. Weightlessness can result in many health problems connected to blood, muscles and bones. It is, therefore, very important that astronauts look after themselves in space.*

## Healthy food

An important part of staying healthy is eating the right food. Space foods are designed with nutrition in mind and are analysed to find out their nutritional content. Menus are prepared in advance to make sure meals provide astronauts with the right balance of carbohydrates, fats, proteins, fibre, vitamins and minerals.

## Food safety

Healthy food is not only nutritious, but is safe to eat. Space food is prepared in a strictly controlled and hygienic environment to prevent the growth of bacteria or mould. If astronauts were struck by food poisoning on a spaceflight, the entire mission could be affected.

**Japanese astronaut Takao Doi (seated, right) and his American counterparts Dominic Gorie (left) and Gregory H. Johnson meet with a dietician to try the food and finalise the menu for their spaceflight.**

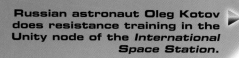

Russian astronaut Oleg Kotov does resistance training in the Unity node of the *International Space Station*.

## Keeping fit

In space, muscles begin to waste away and bones become weaker because the force of gravity is not acting on the body. One way of slowing down this process is to get plenty of exercise. Astronauts spend at least two hours a day working out on specially adapted exercise equipment, such as exercise bikes and treadmills.

## Avoiding infection

Immediately before a spaceflight, astronauts spend several days in **quarantine** so that they are less likely to come into contact with bacteria or viruses that could make them fall sick during the mission. When in space, astronauts regularly wipe the spacecraft's surfaces with a special cleaner to prevent the growth of **microorganisms**.

### Did you know?

To help astronauts avoid infection, the air and water on board the *International Space Station* are purified to a very high standard. The air is a lot cleaner than the air inside a house on Earth and the drinking water is much purer than the water from a kitchen tap.

# FREE TIME IN SPACE

***Astronauts work hard, but they do not work all the time. Like everyone else, they need time to relax and have fun. Mission planners make sure every astronaut gets some free time in their daily schedule.***

## *Relaxing*

One popular pastime in space is looking out the window. This is not surprising as Earth looks beautiful from **orbit** and the view is constantly changing.

Astronauts can also relax by doing some of the things they might do back on Earth, such as reading a book, watching a DVD or chatting with their workmates.

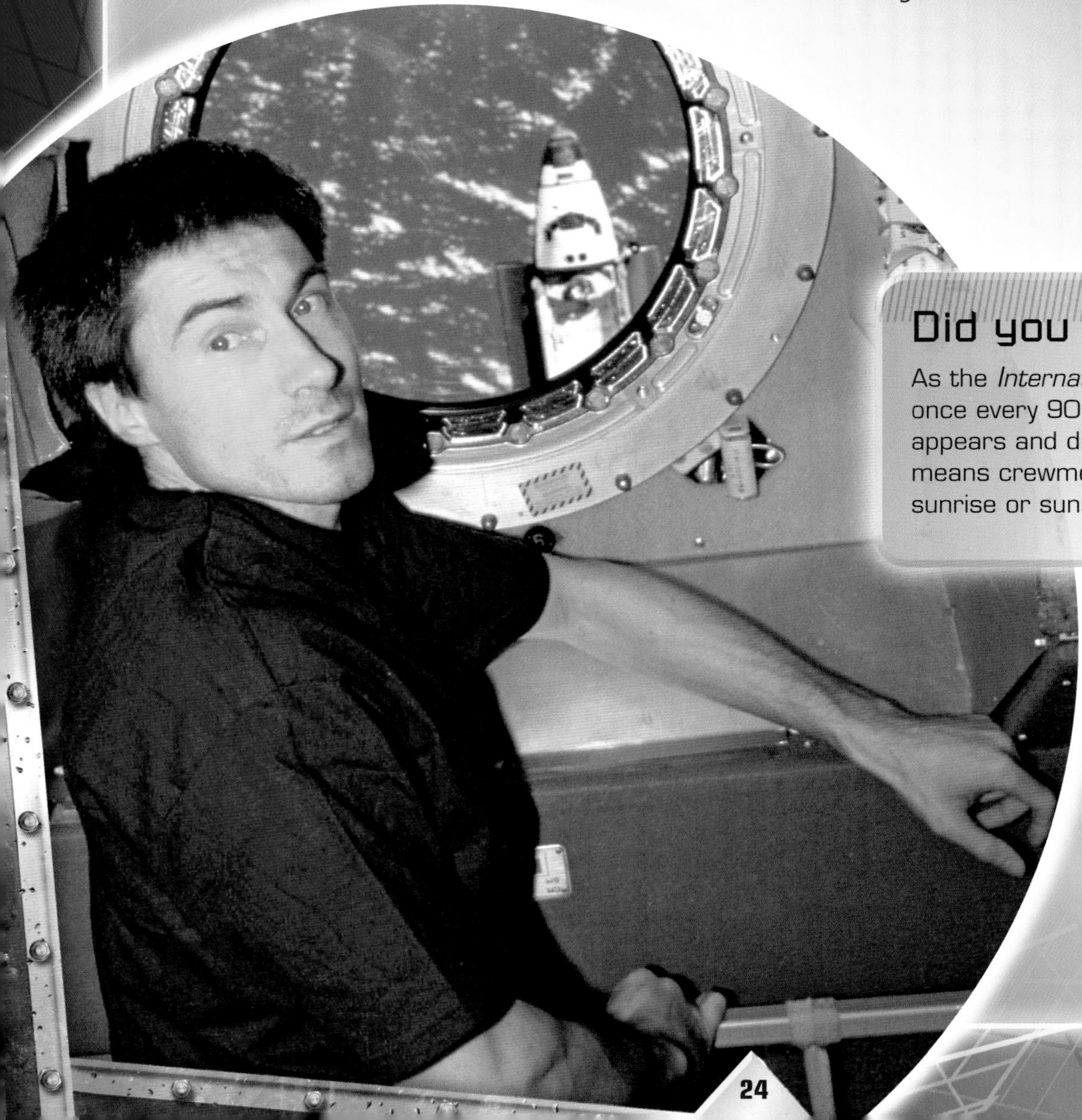

## Did you know?

As the *International Space Station* orbits Earth once every 90 minutes, the Sun repeatedly appears and disappears behind Earth. This means crewmembers see a spectacular sunrise or sunset every 45 minutes.

**Russian astronaut Sergei Krikalev takes in the view from a porthole on board the Zvezda Service Module of the *International Space Station* as the space shuttle *Atlantis* approaches.**

American astronaut Sunita Williams talks to students in Belgium while on board the *International Space Station.*

## Fun and games

Crewmembers can also have fun by playing board games, card games and ball games. A popular game on the *International Space Station* is racing from one end of the station to the other. Astronauts race against the clock rather than against each other because the openings between the modules are so narrow.

## Keeping in touch

During their free time, astronauts can contact friends and family back on Earth via email, radio transmissions and recorded video messages. Keeping in touch is particularly important for the crew of the *ISS*, who may be away from home for up to six months at a time.

### Amateur radio

There is an amateur radio station on board the *International Space Station*, which can communicate with other amateur radio stations on the ground. Astronauts use amateur radio to answer questions from the general public, including students, and to keep in touch with friends and family.

# SCIENTIFIC RESEARCH IN SPACE

*On the International Space Station astronauts have a day job that involves carrying out scientific research through experiments. These experiments are one of the main reasons why the space station was built.*

## Why do research in space?

Research helps scientists prepare for future space missions. Astronauts test the effects of long-term weightlessness on their bodies and develop ways of growing food in space to prepare for missions to Mars. New and improved materials can also be better developed in space due to the effects of **microgravity**.

## Developing new and improved materials

Materials manufactured in microgravity have different physical properties from the same materials manufactured on Earth. These differences can improve the material in some way. The hormone insulin, for example, which is used to treat diabetes, is of a better quality when produced in space. In the future, huge **orbiting** factories and laboratories may manufacture many of the materials we need.

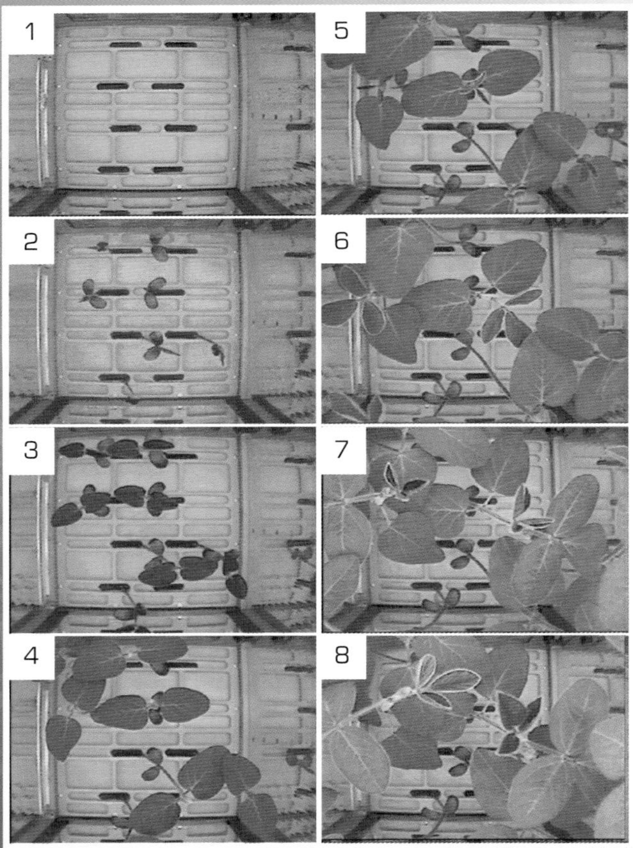


### Did you know?

Special lights called Light Emitting Diodes (LEDs) are used to grow plants in space. They provide enough light for plants to grow well, but use only a small amount of electricity. They save energy by emitting light only at the particular frequencies plants need in order to grow.

**This image shows the growth of soybeans over time in the Advanced Astroculture Plant Growth Chamber of the *International Space Station*.**

This photo shows a Materials International Space Station Experiment (MISSE) attached to the exterior of the station. MISSE collects information on how different materials weather in space.

## *Laboratories on the* International Space Station

The *ISS* has four laboratory modules built by the European Space Agency and the space agencies of the United States, Russia and Japan. Each is fully equipped with everything found in a regular laboratory, including incubators, refrigerators, freezers, gas cupboards, glove boxes and microscopes.

Some experiments do not take place in the laboratories but outside, in the vacuum of space.

The table below shows some of the types of experiments carried out on the *ISS*.

| Type of research | What it does | How it is or will be used |
| --- | --- | --- |
| biological research | finds out how plants and animals react to microgravity and the environment of space | to ensure there is enough food on longer missions in the future |
| Earth observation research | monitors Earth from space | to collect **atmospheric** and climate data for agricultural and environmental research |
| human research | finds out how physical and mental health are affected by spaceflight | to ensure astronauts on longer missions in the future stay healthy |
| physical science research | explores the physics of microgravity | to develop new materials for use in space and on Earth |
| radiation measurement | finds out how much radiation the exterior of the *ISS* receives and how much reaches the crew inside | to calculate possible doses of radiation on a flight to Mars and to design future spacecraft that limit exposure to radiation |

# WORKING OUTSIDE THE SPACECRAFT

*During a spaceflight, not every job can be done from inside the spacecraft. On most missions one or more astronauts perform at least one spacewalk, or Extravehicular Activity (EVA), during which they work outside the spacecraft.*

## Why work outside the spacecraft?

Working in a spacesuit in the vacuum of space is both difficult and dangerous. However, some tasks can only be performed by astronauts working outside the spacecraft. Such tasks include maintaining and repairing the exterior of the spacecraft, monitoring external experiments, and repairing space hardware such as **satellites** and telescopes.

### Did you know?

The longest spacewalk took place during mission STS-102 in 2001. American astronauts James Voss and Susan Helms spent 8 hours and 56 minutes preparing the *International Space Station* to receive a new cargo module.

**American astronaut Stephen Bowen works on parts of the *International Space Station*.**

American astronaut Sunita Williams uses the Pistol Grip Tool while working on the exterior of the *International Space Station* in January 2007.

## The Pistol Grip Tool

Designing the multipurpose Pistol Grip Tool presented many challenges. Not only did it have to do the job of several different power tools, but astronauts had to be able to use it while wearing thick spacesuit gloves. The tool's battery and computer also had to work at extreme temperatures.

## A personal spacecraft

Without a spacesuit, an astronaut would die after only a few minutes of exposure to the hostile environment of space. A spacesuit acts like a mini-spacecraft for one person. It protects the astronaut from extremes of temperature, radiation, bright sunlight and bullet-like **micrometeoroids**. It also provides air to breathe and water to drink.

## Tools in space

One of the most useful space tools is the Pistol Grip Tool, which is an electric drill, screwdriver and spanner. Astronauts also carry a trace gas analyser, which detects any leaking gas or liquid such as oxygen, water or rocket fuel. A robotic crane manoeuvres large objects. It can also pick up astronauts and place them in the right position.

# THE FUTURE OF LIVING AND WORKING IN SPACE

*The most time a single person has spent living and working in space is 437.7 days, which is just over 14 months. In order to make a trip to Mars and back, astronauts will have to spend several years at a time in space. Further into the future, some people may even spend their entire lives in space.*

## Coming soon

More **orbiting** space stations are likely to be built once the *International Space Station* shuts down and, possibly, while it is still operational. NASA is planning to send humans back to the Moon by 2020 and will eventually build a permanently inhabited lunar base, where astronauts and scientists can live and work for many months or even years.

## Looking further ahead

The astronauts who make the first manned flights to Mars will live and work in space for several years, first on board the spacecraft and then on a base that they build on Mars. Eventually, humans may live on other planets and moons in the **solar system**. Children born there might spend their entire lives in space.

**This artist's impression shows what a lunar base might look like. In the background are the living quarters, on the left is a rover and on the right is a landing craft.**

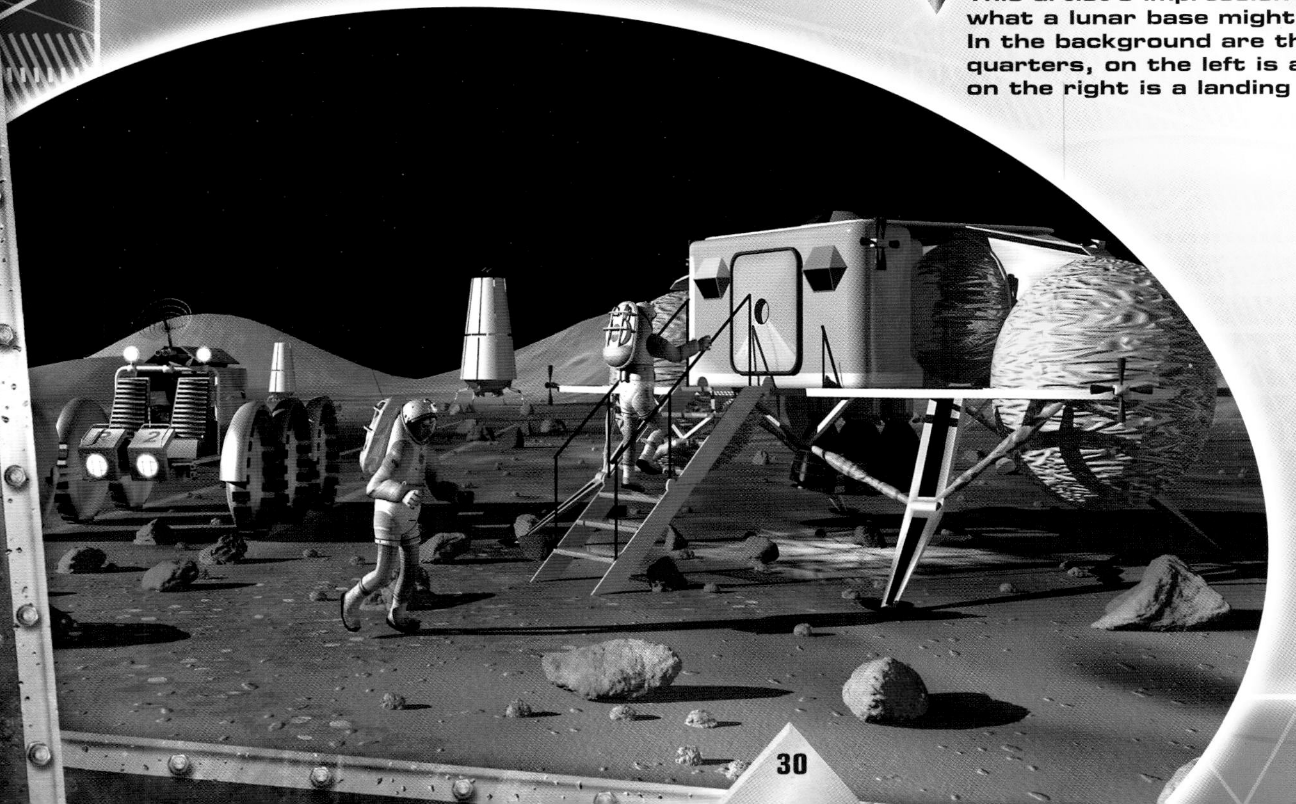

# GLOSSARY

**aerodynamics**
a branch of science that examines the way air interacts with moving objects, such as aircraft

**airlocks**
chambers in a spacecraft that allow astronauts to move in and out of the spacecraft without affecting its air pressure

**allergens**
substances that can cause an allergy, or bad reaction, in some people

**atmosphere**
the layer of gases surrounding a planet, moon or star

**dock**
join one spacecraft to another

**flares**
devices that produce a bright light or coloured smoke, which can be used to attract attention in an emergency

**free fall**
an object is in free fall when it is affected by only gravity and no other force

**gravity**
the strong force that pulls one object towards another

**infrared camera**
a camera that uses infrared radiation rather than visible light to create an image

**ionising radiation**
radiation caused by high-energy electromagnetic waves with very short wavelengths, which can be used to sterilise food

**microgravity**
weightlessness, a phenomenon experienced when orbiting a planet

**micrometeoroid**
a tiny, fast-moving particle of dust or rock commonly found near Earth that can cause damage to spacecraft and spacesuits

**microorganisms**
very tiny living things, such as viruses, bacteria and fungi, which are too small to be seen with the naked eye

**nausea**
the feeling that you are about to vomit

**neutral buoyancy**
a condition that occurs when the weight of an object in water is equal to the weight of the water it displaces, causing the object to neither sink nor rise

**orbited**
followed a curved path around a more massive object while held in place by gravity; the path taken by the orbiting object is its orbit

**parabolic**
describing a type of curve known as a parabola, which is similar to the path taken by an object that is thrown into the air and falls to the ground in a different place

**quarantine**
a period of time when a person is kept away from other people in order to prevent them from catching or spreading disease

**re-entry**
the process of re-entering Earth's atmosphere after a spaceflight

**satellites**
natural or artificial objects in orbit around another body

**solar system**
the Sun and everything in orbit around it, including the planets

**Soviet Union**
a nation that existed from 1922 to 1991, made up of Russia and 14 neighbouring states

**sterilised**
cleaned and germ-free

**virtual reality**
technology that allows a user to interact with a three-dimensional environment simulated by a computer

# INDEX

Sugared
Orange

RECIPES & STORIES
FROM A WINTER IN POLAND

# Sugared Orange

BEATA ZATORSKA & SIMON TARGET

TABULA BOOKS

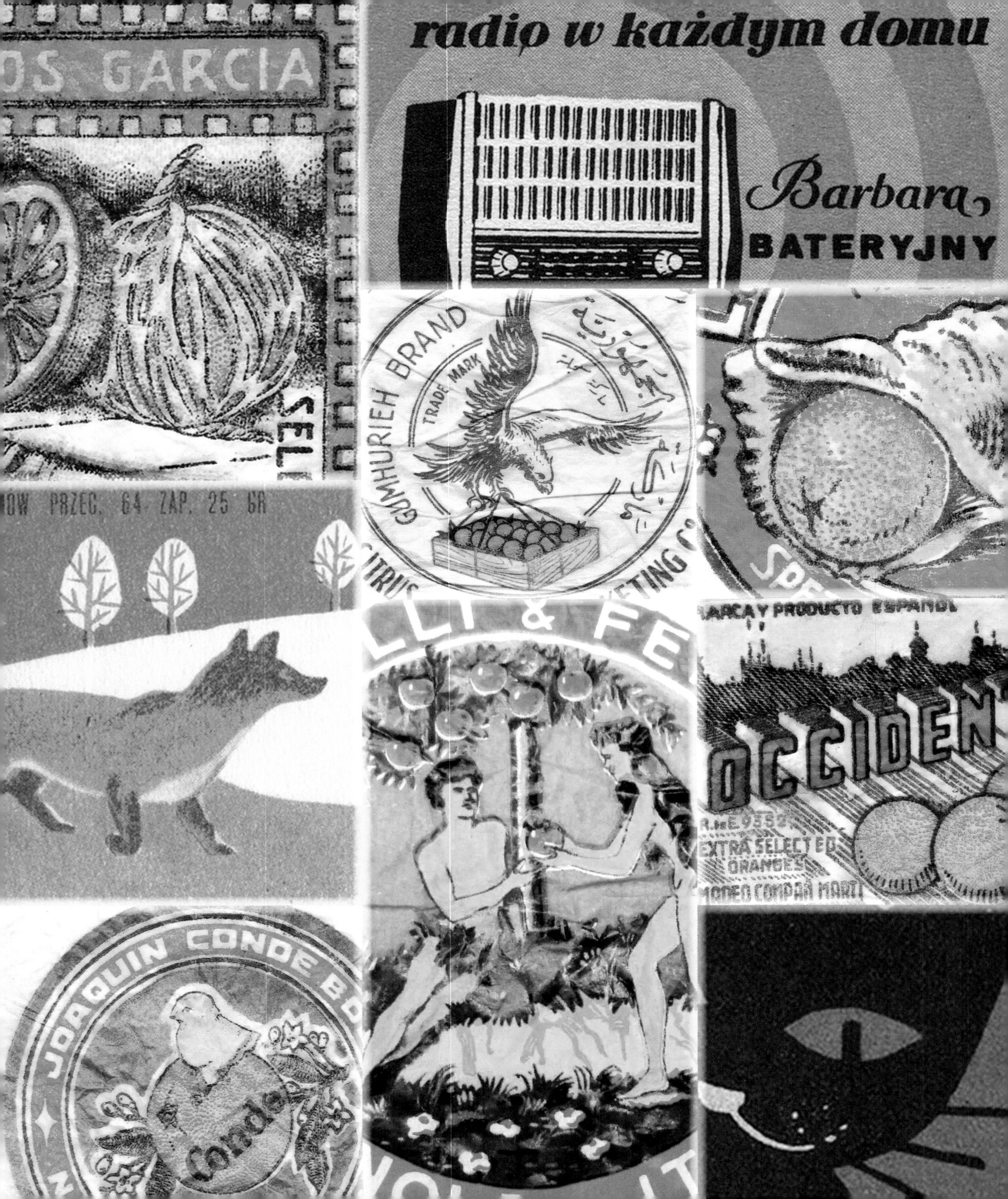
radio w każdym domu
Barbara
BATERYJNY
OS GARCIA
OW PRZEC. 64 ZAP. 25 GR
GUMHURIEH BRAND
TRADE MARK
CITRUS
MARCA Y PRODUCTO ESPANOL
OCCIDEN
EXTRA SELECTED
ORANGES
JOAQUIN CONDE
Conde

# Contents

# Introduction

I slip my hand under the thick lace tablecloth and caress the oak table beneath – my solid, old childhood friend. It feels perfectly smooth as always, not a splinter to smuggle back home. The far end of the table, wedged under the window, was always my kingdom, inhabited by crocheted dolls and bears, walled off by boxes of wax crayons and stacks of coloured paper. At least twice a week it had to be cleared – when my grandmother made pierogi. She worked and rolled out the dough across the floured wooden surface, then with an upturned cup cut out neat circles. She made them into pasta pockets with different fillings – potato and farm cheese, minced beef, fresh blueberries in summer – but at Christmas, always with cabbage and mushrooms. She used to give me my own small lump of dough to play with, to flatten with her giant rolling pin, and cut out stars, flowers, and smiling moons. All this fun to the sounds of Chopin and cosmic radiation hissing through the woven speaker grill of the radio. It is 30 years since my grandmother died. The time has dried only my outside tears.

A month ago I stood outside our Sydney home, melting in a summer heatwave. I hid in the shade of a eucalyptus tree, waiting for a taxi to take me and my husband to the airport. The Sri Lankan driver smiled at us in the rear view mirror, confessing he had never seen snow. He dropped us at the airport's sliding doors, into a crowd of desperate smokers kissing their cigarettes goodbye.

OPPOSITE "Winter" by Stanisław Kamocki, 1910.

This frosty evening I stand under a leafless linden tree in front of my grandmother's house, in the heart of a small mountain village in Poland's Karkonosze Mountains. The tree's dark dry branches crack the milky sky above into broken eggshell. I seem to be melting again, as my Aussie sheep's skin boots sink into three feet of snow.

It is Christmas Eve and I sit at the table across from my elderly aunt. The wrinkles on her hand match the deep crevices in the crystal wine glass she holds. I feel like kissing her hand in gratitude for making pierogi tonight. I have been dreaming of her dumplings ever since I got on the plane in Australia.

At midnight I shall walk to mass in the village church to receive Christmas blessings, although I feel already blessed by my family's affectionate welcome. The old oak table is beautifully decorated tonight, silver and crystal-ware competing for sparkles in the candlelight. And there is an extra place laid for an unexpected guest. My grandmother once explained this old Polish tradition... a spare setting at the table for a traveller, gypsy, or lost mountain walker who might wander in unexpectedly on Christmas Eve.

Suddenly there is a knock. I sprint down the steep, stone stairs to open the front door and run out. There is no-one there. I spin around and feel snow flakes melt on my duty-free, south sea pearl necklace. And at that moment I feel my grandmother is here, teasing me that I am the lost-in-the-mountains-gypsy-traveller, who has arrived on Christmas Eve to eat pierogi. I step back in, shutting the heavy door. My silver-haired uncle mutters something about pruning the old cherry tree branch that bangs against the roof in the wind. Dear old man, must be losing his senses.

FOLLOWING PAGE (inset) "Roses and Chamomile" by Władysław Ślewiński, 1908.

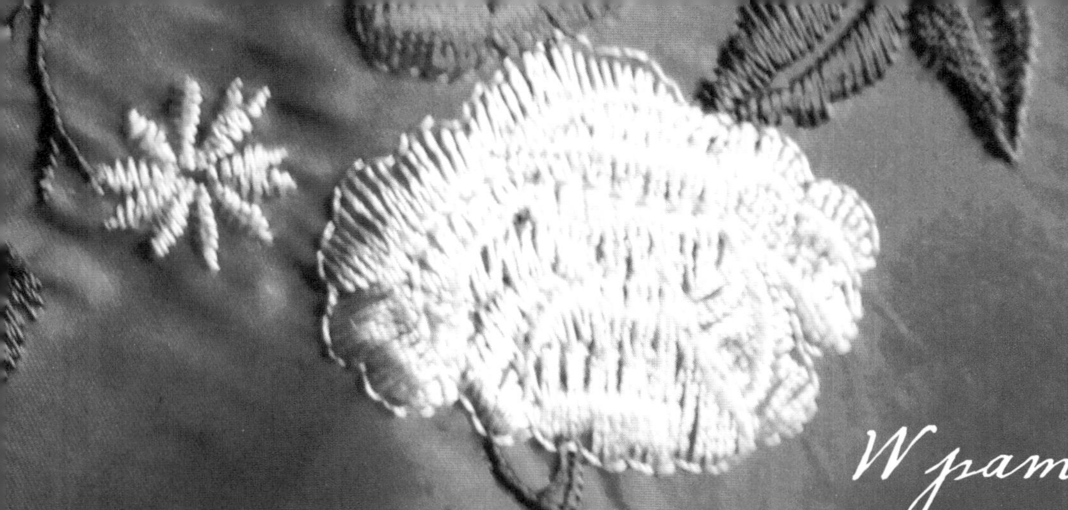

# Lines in Zofia's autograph album

Don't ask a poem of me, Zosia sweet,
for when to our homeland our Zosia will come,
there every flower shall verses repeat,
there every star shall a song to her hum.
Before the blooms fade, before the stars fall,
listen – these poets are best of them all.

The azure stars, and the flowers so red,
an entire poem will for you compose;
I would just copy whatever they said,
for I have learned all my chatter from those:
for there, where Ikwa its silver course runs,
a child, like Zosia, I too played there once.

A visitor now, I sojourn afar,
ill-fortune followed, wherever I went,
bring to me, Zosia the light of one star,
do bring back, Zosia one such flower's scent
my youth I crave again to be given!
Bring it back for me – as if from heaven.

# W pamiętniku Zofii Bobrówny

*Niechaj mię Zośka o wiersze nie prosi,*
*Bo kiedy Zośka do ojczyzny wróci,*
*To każdy kwiatek powie wiersze Zosi,*
*Każda jej gwiazdka piosenkę zanuci.*
*Nim kwiat przekwitnie, nim gwiazdeczka zleci,*
*Słuchaj – bo to są najlepsi poeci.*

*Gwiazdy błękitne, kwiateczki czerwone*
*Będą ci całe poemata składać.*
*Ja bym to samo powiedział, co one,*
*Bo ja się od nich nauczyłem gadać;*
*Bo tam, gdzie Ikwy srebrne fale płyną,*
*Byłem ja niegdyś, jak Zośka, dzieciną.*

*Dzisiaj daleko pojechałem w gości*
*I dalej mię los nieszczęśliwy goni.*
*Przywieź mi, Zośko, od tych gwiazd światłości,*
*Przywieź mi, Zośko, z tamtych kwiatów woni,*
*Bo mi zaprawdę odmłodnieć potrzeba.*
*Wróć mi więc z kraju taką – jakby z nieba.*

Juliusz Słowacki, 1844 (trans. M. Weyland)

# A CHILDHOOD IN POLAND

*I have spent 30 years in Australia and learnt to love my sunburnt country; but I was born in Poland where I lived for the first 18 years of my life. My childhood days were divided between my grandmother Józefa's house, in a remote village in the*

*I have spent 30 years in Australia and learnt to love my sunburnt country, but I was born in Poland where I lived for the first 18 years of my life. My childhood days were divided between my grandmother Józefa's house, in a remote village in the*

*foothills of the Karkonosze Mountains, and my parents' apartment in Jelenia Góra, where I went to school. My village friends could never forgive my urban connections and "worldliness", so I was nicknamed Miastowa (the girl from the city), making sure I had to try extra hard to be a part of their games in the village forests. Colourful lollipops bought in town were usually enough to soften their contempt for the metropolis only 12 kilometres away.*

Beata's grandmother 'Mama Druga' with her son Jasiu (Beata's uncle).

# Mama Druga

*My grandmother Józefa, whom I called Mama Druga (my 'second mum') was a war widow. Her husband Rudolf was killed during the Second World War in 1943, aged 30. She was only 26 when in 1945, holding two young children in her arms, she travelled on a train from the Polish eastern borderlands, the Kresy, to Lower Silesia.*

Many Polish families had to be moved from the Kresy, which had become part of Soviet Russia. They were resettled in the western part of Poland that belonged to Germany before the War. Here my grandmother, her two younger sisters and aging parents were allocated a German farmhouse, where my great-grandfather Dimitri found some carpentry tools. He soon opened a cart, wheel, and barrel-making workshop that allowed villagers to restart farming and the community to prosper in the years of post-war poverty and hunger.

In 1948, with the start of the Cold War, Dimitri's business was shut down. Punished for making a profit, Dimitri was pronounced an enemy of the state and banned from ever working again. For years after, local people came knocking on his door at night, with gifts of vegetables, fruit, and

OPPOSITE Beata aged 4.

eggs, begging him to repair their farm equipment. He always helped, all the while fearing that the next knock on the door would be the secret police. He was never arrested, but sentenced instead to long years of boredom, frustration, and financial problems.

My grandmother Józefa, a former teacher, was allowed to work as a chef in a nearby castle, which had been transformed after the War into a holiday resort for workers and their children. Józefa loved her job and created tasty dishes for her guests, people she didn't even know. She poured her heart into her work, treating the holidaymakers as her family, explaining away her enthusiasm as traditional Lwowian hospitality. There were always fresh flowers on the tables, which I often had to collect from the village meadows. In winter, I found small pine branches and dried pine cones in the forests surrounding the castle to use as essential table decorations.

Józefa sprinkled dry rose petals onto her guests' *kisiel* (hot fruit jelly), smuggled wild blueberries into their *pierogi*, chopped fresh dill over their mashed potatoes, and spiced

ABOVE Beata's great grand parents, Julia and Dimitri.

RIGHT Evacuation order issued by the authorities to Mama Druga and her family.

RIGHT INSET Beata's grandparents, Józefa and Rudolf in Lwów at the onset of the War.

22495

ПРЕДСТАВ...

Дата ...

Реф...

Główny Pełnomocnik
Головний Уповноважений

Tymczasowego Rządu Narodowego
Тимчасового Національного Уряду

Rzeczypospolitej Polskiej
Польської Республіки

4 вересня 1945

# KARTA EWAKUACYJNA
## Евакуаційний лист

Wydano obywatelowi Bajor Józefa c. Dymitra r. 1917 roku
Дано громадянинові Баєр Юзефа Дмитрівна року народж.

mieszkańcowi wsi (miasta) ... obwodu
жителю села (міста) ... області

jako dowód, że za zezwoleniem Głównego Pełnomocnika Tymczasowego Rządu Naro...
в тому, що він за дозволом Головного Уповноваженого Тимчасового Націона...

dowego dla ewakuacji z terytorium Ukraińskiej SRR
ного Уряду Польської Республіки по евакуації з території Української РСР.

ewakuuje się do ... powiatu ...
евакуюється до ... волості

województwa ...
воєводства Польщі.

Wraz z nim ewakuuje się następujących ...
З ним евакуюються такі члени його сі...

Nazwisko, imię, imię ojca
Прізвище, ім'я та по батькові

Bajor Jan s. Rudolfa
Bajor Lidia c. Rudolfa
Hlotów Janina c. Dymitra
Schneider Elżbieta c. Stefana

Zapomogi ...

their pale tea with wild cherry syrup. She made them lift their faces from their plates with surprise and amazement by the sudden appearance of colour and perfume in such mundane communist times. Józefa's cooking became legendary and many workers applied to return to her castle instead of the more popular holiday destinations on the Baltic Sea.

She also cooked at home for our family, with most of the fresh produce coming from the garden. In winter, we ate preserves that she had painstakingly made through the preceding seasons. By the first snow fall our cellar was filled with multi-coloured jars of fruit and vegetables. There were no food shortages in her kitchen, and she could always come up with an imaginative recipe, no matter which five-yearly communist-party economic plan the country was enduring. When the pantry was finally empty she would cook something unusual, like a wild sorrel soup, from sorrel that grew in the village meadows, with hard-boiled eggs laid by one of Julia's precious chickens. And for dessert she baked apples, freshly picked from the grass below the apple tree's branches. She filled them with jam made from the petals of the wild rose bushes outside our front door. I loved her fancy food, unaware we were living in very un-fancy times.

In the winter Józefa made sugared orange peel and glass jars of it took centre stage in her pantry among the humble preserves of gooseberries and rhubarb. The perfume of orange peel infused my brain with dreams of tropical lands, orange trees, and exotic adventures for when I grew up.

It was Józefa's parents Julia and Dimitri who took care of our farm garden and orchard, cursing the poor Silesian soil, whilst dreaming of the large orange pumpkins they had grown back in the Kresy. Dimitri died in 1965, failing to convert to communism on his deathbed, leaving Julia bereaved and wearing black for the rest of her life.

MINSK
MOSKWA II
PRAHA
DŁ
280
260
240
200
LANDAU
NÜRNBERG
OPOLE
ŁODZ
MTE CARLO
LUXEMBOURG II
BIAŁYSTOK
NOVI SAD
WROCŁAW
KRAKOW
HÖRBY
ZAGREB
BRATISLAVA
KATOWICE
DRESDEN
BERLIN
HAMBURG
PARIS I
ROMA X
SOFIA
ŚR
1600
1400
1200
1000
900
800
KR

PAN TADEUSZ
Tadeusz Dołęga-Mostowicz
HELENA MNISZEK
TRĘDOWATA
TRĘDOWATA
LISTY Z PODRÓŻY DO AMERYKI
Henryk Sienkiewicz
H. Mniszek ORDYNAT MICHOROWSKI
HELENA MNISZEK SFINKS
RODZIEWICZÓWNA
wiersze
Chopin

Julia spent the next 15 years attending to her chickens, gardening, and reading. She turned two of Dimitri's massive oak cartwheels into a chicken roost, changing the fragrant straw regularly and whispering tender Slavic words to her birds to encourage them to lay more eggs. Julia was famous for growing poppies and her poppy seed was bartered for other local produce. I loved the conspiratorial walks with her through the village, wicker baskets loaded with poppy seed bags, knocking on farmers' doors and returning with jars of butter, cream, and honey.

In her spare time, Julia devoured books, magazines, her grandchildrens' textbooks, and even phonebooks, when we failed to find her something new to read. She spoke five languages, and read to me the Russian children's magazine *Murzilka*. She tried to impress on me the importance of learning foreign languages, advice I ignored right up to when I landed in Australia, not speaking any English. Through the kitchen window I often watched her head off to the nearby church in the evening. Walking fast, dressed in her black dress with a black scarf wrapped around her head, she seemed happy to have another day behind her and be one day closer to the time when she was finally allowed to join her beloved Dimitri in the "Kresy above the clouds".

Great-grandmother Julia.

Julia's daughter, my grandmother Józefa, adored the Karkonosze Mountains and took me on long walks through the hilly fields around our village. She taught me the use of many plants and wildflowers in cooking and in healing. She was my white witch and I was her apprentice. Her teaching inspired me to become a doctor.

I left Poland in 1981 with my family. Józefa was too sick to travel with us. I promised her that I would return soon, but I was never to see her again. She died a few weeks after what was to be our last embrace. My broken promise still haunts me in my dreams, until her smiling face finally appears, and kisses me goodnight.

It took me 20 years to pluck up the courage to return to her house and garden and to read her name on a grey granite stone in the old village cemetery. I had gone back with the encouragement of my English husband Simon. It was an enchanted summer, with long days, fragrant with wild roses and sundried hay. Simon took many photographs for me to take back to Australia and I wrote my memoirs for him. That was how our first book *Rose Petal Jam* came about.

I felt however that I hadn't finished my Polish story yet, and kept writing. We returned to Poland, this time in winter. We travelled for weeks, across the snow-covered land, collecting stories, photographs, recipes, and Christmas wishes. We went to Warsaw and Kraków, Lublin and Łódź, the Mazury Lakes, and Europe's oldest forest near Białowieża. We paused for Christmas with my Polish family, delighting our relatives by eating their food, emptying their fridge and pantry, and loading our car with even more supplies for more winter travel around Poland. We felt safe on icy winding roads, looked after by my Mama Druga, who watched us from behind snowy clouds beneath the heavens.

Grandmother Józefa as a young woman in Lwów.

*The apples from our orchard were stored in a cool cellar, ready to be eaten throughout the winter. They were placed neatly in rows, without touching each other to prevent bruising. My job was to inspect them regularly for any signs of aging. Any with shrivelled skin were picked out for baking. I tried to find as many as possible, occasionally deliberately scratching an apple, so more dessert had to be made. My grandmother prepared a simple rose petal jam filling by crushing sugar with wild rose petals in a stone bowl.*

JABŁKA PIECZONE Z DŻEMEM Z RÓŻY

# Baked Apples with Rose Petal Jam

SERVES 6

- 6 cooking (baking) apples
- 6 tablespoons rose petal jam (or any thick jam)

Preheat the oven to 180°C (350°F).

Wash the apples, then slice off the tops horizontally, about 1 cm (½ in) from the stems, to form lids.

Remove the apple cores.

Put a tablespoon of jam inside each apple, replace the lids, then bake the apples on a buttered baking tray for 30 minutes.

When you remove the apples from the oven, scoop up the melted jam from the tray and drizzle it over the apples.

Serve hot.

# *Sugared Orange Peel*

*In winter, pyramids of imported oranges appeared in the windows of shops in Polish towns. Long queues snaked along city roads, with people waiting patiently to buy one or two of these rare fruit for Christmas.*

Each orange was individually wrapped in fine tissue paper imprinted with exotic images of palm trees, camels, or voluptuous, smiling women. I knew the fruit arrived in large crates from tropical countries where the sun itself looked like a plump orange. And I knew that is where the storks from our roof flew away to each winter.

My grandmother Józefa, uncharacteristically accepting of fruit "brought from the city", used every bit of each precious orange, and candied the peel. However the aromatic tissue wrapping paper was mine. I used to fold it into bookmarks, and soon my books smelt of orange – for me, the true scent of a Polish Christmas.

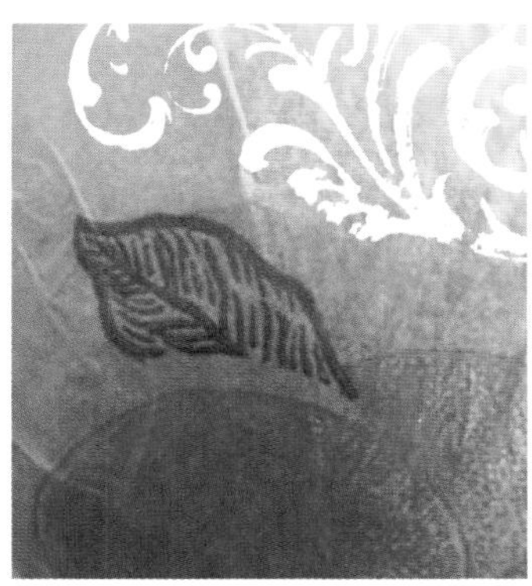

IMPORTADO DE ESPAÑA
HET SPAANSCHE MEISJE
IK HEB DE FIJNSTE BLOESEM
EXTRA SELECTED SINAASAPPELEN
SPECIAAL
JUAN PITARCH CAPELLA
"PRIMERA JUGADA"
EXTRA SELECTA
NARANJAS VALENCIA
MARCA REGISTRADA
Buon Anno
Bonne Noël
Merry Christmas and a Happy New Year
Ein frohes
BLAUES HUHN
BENIARJO-(VALENCIA)
SAFTIG UND SÜSS
Feliz Navidad y Año Nuevo
Spania
niobe
Producido en España
SANTA LUCIA - AGRICULTURA IND & COM. S.A
LARANJAS SELECIONADAS
BEST SELECTED CITRUS FRUIT
PRODUCE
SÃO PAULO
FONDI(LT)

TELLI & FERRARI
VIGNOLA · ITALIA
ALCIRA
IMPORTADO DE ESPAÑA
GATO NEGRO
SELECTA
AGRUNA
VALENCIA
MARCA
REGISTRADA
Ausar
LA CLÉMENTINE DE MON ENFANCE
DEPUIS 1926
Teddy
MARCA
DEPOSITATA
SALVATORE RACITI-PATERNO
BLAZE
R. E. 24.339
Sociedad de Exportacion nº 1
ARTANA
انتاج
جمهورية مصر العربية
EL WADI BEST SELECTED CITRUS FRUITS
PRODUCE OF EGYPT
TREATED

*My grandmother hid the glass jars of sugared orange peel on the highest, unreachable pantry shelves. No chances were taken in our house with a candy-loving child about. Even in Australia (where oranges seem to grow in front of every house) I need to hide these tempting treats. My children love them, leaving behind empty jars bespeckled with sugar crystals. As they grow taller it becomes harder to find shelves high enough on which to conceal my precious peel.*

## KANDYZOWANA SKÓRKA Z POMARAŃCZY

# *Sugared Orange Peel*

MAKES ABOUT 50 PIECES

4 sweet oranges
1.2 l (5 cups) water
675 g (1½ lb) caster (superfine) sugar
extra sugar for dusting

Wash the oranges carefully to remove any wax. Using a sharp knife, score each orange from stem to tip into 4 equal segments, cutting the skin but not the fruit inside.

Carefully remove the peel from the orange in 4 pieces.Use a knife to scrape off as much of the bitter white pith as you can. Cut each piece of peel vertically into 3 or 4 strips about 1 cm (½ in) wide.

In a large saucepan, dissolve the sugar in the water by heating gently and stirring continuously. Bring the sugar syrup to the boil, then add the orange peel. Simmer uncovered on a low heat for about 2 hours, checking from time to time that the peel is still covered with the sugar syrup. During this time the liquid will reduce until it barely covers the peel.

Once cooked, lift out the peel with a slotted spoon, drain, and allow to cool.

Dust the orange peel pieces by rolling them while still sticky in a bowl of sugar, then spread them out individually on baking paper to set.

Once dried, the peel can be stored in jars in a dry place for at least 3 months. It can be used for many different Christmas recipes for sweetness.

*My family recipe for this sugared orange cake is very easy to make. This cake is moist and light in texture. I challenge you to eat only one slice.*

## CIASTO POMARAŃCZOWE

# *Sugared Orange Cake*

SERVES 6 TO 8

FOR THE CAKE
2 eggs
finely grated rind and juice of 1 medium orange
300g (10 oz) self raising flour
160ml (¼ pint) vegetable oil
300g (10 oz) natural yoghurt (Greek style)
400g (14 oz) caster (superfine) sugar

FOR THE TOPPING
1 orange sliced thinly
225 g (8 oz) granulated sugar
150g (5 oz) icing (powdered) sugar plus extra for decoration
1 tbs orange juice

Preheat oven to 180°C (350°F). Combine eggs, yoghurt, oil, sugar, orange juice and rind. Sift in the flour, mix gently then pour into a greased 22 cm (9 in) baking tin. Bake for 30 mins or until light brown and cooked when tested with a skewer.

Remove cake from tin, allow to cool and make a frosting by mixing the icing sugar with 1 tablespoon orange juice. Add a few more drops of water if needed to make it really smooth. Spread over top of cake.

Preheat oven to 200°C (400°F). Melt the granulated sugar in 50 ml (2 fl oz) water, add the orange slices and simmer for 20 minutes. Drain the orange slices then arrange on a baking paper on a baking tray. Bake in the oven for 20 minutes.

Allow to cool then place sugared orange slices on top of iced cake, dusting with extra icing sugar.

*Heidi is my neighbour in Sydney. We go to concerts together and fuss about modern interpretations of Bach. We were born in the same city, but in two different countries. We accept that we each have a different name for our home town, she says Hirschberg, I say Jelenia Góra. Both mean "deer mountain"– after the wild deer that*

*Jelenia Góra*

*roam the surrounding forests. We went to high schools in the same building but 40 years apart, she to the German school, I to the Polish. Now both German and Polish can be learnt in that school, languages Heidi and I like to mix when we walk home, arm in arm, from the Sydney Opera House.*

PN-62/D-94061

THE ARRIVAL OF WINTER

*Abandoning a bright and hot Australian summer for a dark and chilly Europe seems inexplicable to my friends, but I am longing to be in Poland in the early days of winter, to feel the excitement of Christmas approaching. During the long plane trip I stare*

*Abandoning a bright and hot Australian summer for a dark and chilly Europe seems inexplicable to my friends, but I am longing to be in Poland in the early days of winter, to feel the excitement of Christmas approaching. During the long plane trip I stare*

WILK

out the window, half expecting to see storks flying the other way in search of sun. I let the first snow petals melt on my outstretched hand outside Warsaw airport, inaugurating our winter journey. When I walk through the streets of Polish towns and villages my eyes are veiled by a chiffon of snow, but I follow the scent of dried mushrooms and sugared orange coming through doors and windows. I want to knock on those doors and call out: 'Let me in! Let me in! I have been away for many years, but I know there is a spare place at your Christmas table!'

"Warsaw Old Town Square at Night" by Józef Pankiewicz, 1892.

U
BARSSA

# *Warszawa*

*I first saw Warsaw as a child in 1968 through the window of a school bus. The buildings seemed so high and streets so frantically busy with cars and trams.*

I admired our capital and was ready to return year after year to visit the Pałac Kultury, and the Wilanów and Łazienki palaces. As an adult I heard many stories about the city from my patients that settled in Australia after World War 2. Their tales of pre-war Warsaw and the Uprisal only deepen my affection for the town. In Sydney I check the weather in Warsaw every day, not to miss the moment when a 25 degree 'heatwave' makes the kids jump into the Syrenka fountain or minus 25 arrests the Vistula River on its way to the Baltic Sea.

ABOVE Warsaw Royal Castle.

The 21st century Warsaw puts on a fairy tale spectacle at Christmas. All the lights switch on the moment grey dusk threatens the city. Garlands of sparkling lights join street lamps, statues, and leafless trees in a Christmas conga line that traverses back and forth through city alleys, parks, and squares. Nowy Świat, Krakowskie Przedmieście, the Stare and Nowe Miasto are all suspended in a milky way of twinkling stars. This light show brightens the saddest of faces and makes dazzled young children look up and trip over their parents' boots.

A maze of stalls crowd the old town. Warmly dressed, cheerful sellers remove their thick gloves to serve homemade Christmas treats. My great grandmother Julia would be shocked by all this food available to eat way before Christmas. I hope she will forgive me and understand I am tasting purely for research, and am writing a book she hasn't already read.

ABOVE The Syrenka (Mermaid) statue, a symbol of Warsaw, in the Old Town. RIGHT "New World" Street in Winter by Władysław Podkowiński, 1892.

FOLLOWING PAGES Wilanów Palace, Warsaw

David
Sèvres

*The sweet and spicy vapours of heated wine that is served in so many Warsaw cafes are enough to make you tipsy. Drinking mulled wine from street stalls kept us immune to cold during long walks round old Warsaw.*

## GRZANE WINO

# Hot Mulled Wine

MAKES 10 GLASSES

peel and juice of 1 lime
peel and juice of 1 orange
250 g (9 oz) caster (superfine) sugar
2 teaspoons freshly grated ginger
12 cloves
1 stick cinnamon
2 bay leaves
1 whole nutmeg, halved and grated
2 bottles / 1.5 l (2½ pints) dry red wine
1 extra orange for serving, if desired

Place the orange and lime peel in a large saucepan. Add sugar, orange and lime juice, grated ginger, cloves, cinnamon stick, bay leaves, and nutmeg. Stir over a low heat to melt the sugar, adding a dash of the wine to keep it liquid.

When the sugar has melted, bring to the boil and simmer for 10 minutes.

Remove from heat and allow the liquid to cool a little before stirring in the rest of the wine. Warm gently until it is piping hot, but not boiling.

Strain liquid before serving into warmed mugs or glasses. For decoration, slice the extra orange thinly, cutting each slice into quarters to float on top of your wine.

13

czerwony
6zł
beetroot soup
coffee
herbata
6zł
tea

Cena 14zł/kg
CHLEB
Z DYNIA

PIEROGI
Cena 41,-
KIEŁBASA
SEREK
czerwony
beetroot
soup

# Lublin

*The renaissance city of Lublin feels mysterious on a cold winter's evening. Bathed in honey-yellow light, narrow streets and passages spiral up to the old city square where the Christmas markets are held.*

The town houses on the square are meticulously restored, many bearing plaques to commemorate famous Poles who were one-time Lublin residents. One of them, Henryk Wieniawski, was a 19th-century composer and violinist whose two concertos I knew well from Polish radio broadcasts in the 1960s.

My husband  points to a Polish inscription on an ancient wall. I struggle to translate for him, for this is Old Polish, the words of a renaissance scholar and humanist from the 16th century. I do my best: "Keep peace with all your neighbours and there will be no need for war". Here it is, a message some 500 years old, but one yet to be discovered by today's world leaders. I suggest a new UN Security Council meeting should be held on Lublin's old market square. There will be only one resolution, already inscribed on the wall to make it easy to remember.

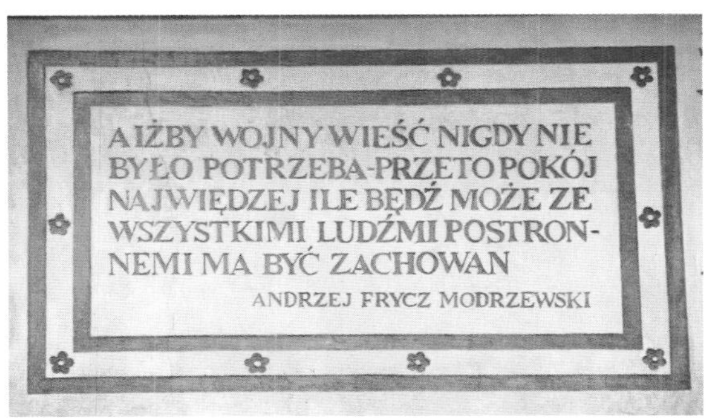

We are soon in a queue for food in one of Lublin's street markets. The aroma of wine, mushrooms, onions, and gingerbread is too much to resist while trying to decipher medieval inscriptions. I can hear Russian, Polish, Lithuanian, and Ukrainian all spoken in the old market, tongues fusing together into one slavic Esperanto, reminding us we are close to Poland's eastern border. There is an exciting mix of across-the-border neighbours and their cuisines all gathered under Modrzewski's sign. We eat kapuśniaki (savoury buns filled with cabbage, see page 67) and bite into a cheesecake made with pearl barley (kaszak lubelski, see page 68), buying another 2 kg slab to carry back to our hotel in case we get hungry at night. I recognize all these delicacies: my grandmother Józefa, who grew up not far from here, in Lwów, cooked them all.

RIGHT Christmas market stall in the Old Town selling hand-made Lublin lace. FOLLOWING PAGES: The magnificent frescoes depicting the life of Jesus on the ceiling of the 13th-century Holy Trinity Chapel, Lublin Castle.

mała restauracja
Rynek 14

*Pearl barley, like snow petals, adorns this vegetable soup. It lends it a thick and creamy texture making a hearty winter dish.*

KRUPNIK

# *Pearl Barley Soup*

ENOUGH FOR 4

- 1 small onion
- 2 large carrots
- ½ stalk celery
- 2 small chicken wings
- c. 3 l (about 5 pints) water
- 1 large potato
- 1 parsnip
- 4 dried porcini mushrooms
- 200 g (7 oz) pearl barley (kasza jęczmienna perłowa)
- 2 tablespoons chopped fresh dill
- 2 tablespoons chopped fresh parsley

Peel and finely chop the onion, carrots, celery and parsnip. Place in a pot with the chicken wings, mushrooms, barley, water, and half the dill and parsley. Bring to the boil, and simmer for about an hour.

Peel and chop the potato into 2 cm (¾ in) cubes. Add to the soup. Cook for 10–15 minutes until the potato has softened, but is still whole. If the soup is too thick you can always add a little more water.

Season with salt and pepper. Before serving, remove the chicken bones and sprinkle the rest of the dill and parsley on top.

*The smell of freshly baked cabbage buns wafted across the snowy fields where I played as a child, luring me back to my grandmother's house. I was followed by an army of red-cheeked village kids, with huge appetites. We gulped hot steamy buns quickly, so we could run off and disappear into the frozen landscape outside my grandmother's kitchen window.*

KAPUŚNIAKI

# Savoury Buns with Cabbage & Mushrooms

MAKES ABOUT 18 BUNS

FOR THE FILLING
- 150g (5 oz) fresh mushrooms
- 1 kg (approx 2lb) jar pickled sauerkraut cabbage
- 1 onion
- 2 tsp butter for frying

FOR THE PASTRY
- 500g (1lb) plain (all purpose) flour
- 75g (3 oz) unsalted butter
- 200ml (about half a pint) full cream milk
- 1 tbs caster (superfine) sugar
- 2 eggs
- 50g fresh yeast or 21g (3× 7 g or ¼ oz packets) dried yeast
- 2 tbs caraway seeds

Rinse and drain the sauerkraut cabbage. Place it in a large saucepan, cover with water, bring to the boil, then simmer for 5 minutes. Drain well, squeeze excess water out with a muslin cloth (cheesecloth). Chop roughly.

Chop onion and mushrooms. Fry in butter in a large pan. Add cabbage and fry together on a medium heat for 5 minutes to reduce the moisture content. Season with salt and pepper.

To make the pastry, mix yeast with 2 tablespoons of flour, the sugar and about 100ml (¼ pint) milk at room temperature. Use a fork to blend into a smooth paste. Add more milk if necessary. Leave this yeast mix to stand for 15 minutes.

Melt the butter, and allow to cool slightly. Sift flour and add with the melted butter to the yeast mix. Add one egg, lightly beaten and a pinch of salt. Add the rest of the milk slowly, using a food processor with a dough hook to blend the mixture. When the mixture is ready it will not be sticky, and will fall freely from the dough hook. Leave the dough covered somewhere warm to rise. It will double or triple in size in 20 minutes.

Pre-heat the oven to 180°C (350°F). Gently roll out dough into a square shape on a floured board to 5mm (¼ in) thickness. Cut into 12cm (5 in) squares. Place 1-2 tablespoons of filling on each square then fold over and pinch the edges to seal together. Gently roll into an elongated bun shape. Place buns on baking paper on a baking tray, at least 5cm (2 in) apart. Leave for 15 minutes to rise some more, then paint with the remaining egg (lightly beaten) and sprinkle with salt and caraway seeds. Bake for 45 minutes or until they are golden brown.

*Kaszak can be savoury, made with buckwheat and onion, but I prefer it sweet. My grandmother baked it in a loaf tin, then sliced it like bread for breakfast, spreading fruit konfitura on top just in case it was not sweet enough for me. (She always said she had yet to invent a recipe that was too sweet for her sweet-toothed grandchild.)*

## KASZAK LUBELSKI

# Lublin Barley Cake

MAKES 1 LOAF OR CAKE

- 500g (1lb) "farm" cheese
- 100g (4 oz) pearl barley (kasza jęczmienna perłowa)
- 1 litre (about 2 pints) water
- 2 eggs, beaten
- 50g (2 oz) potato flour
- 150 g (5 oz) caster (superfine)sugar
- 1 tsp vanilla essence
- 6 pieces of sugared orange peel, chopped (optional) and/or
- 50g sultanas (golden raisins)
- for Sugared Orange Peel see page 32

Add the barley into about 1 litre of boiling salted water. Cook for 15–20 minutes, stirring occasionally. Drain and rinse with cold water, so the barley grains separate.

Pre-heat the oven to 180 C.

Use a fork to break up the cheese in a mixing bowl. Add the barley, one beaten egg, potato flour, sugar and vanilla essence. Add the sugared orange peel or sultanas if desired. Mix together well.

Line a greased loaf tin 24 × 14 × 7 cm (9½ × 5½ × 3 in) with baking paper. Pour in the mixture and paint the top with the other beaten egg. Bake for 40 minutes.

Remove from oven and let cool for about an hour before cutting into thick slices and serving with a glass of milk.

POLSKA 2,50 ZŁ
1000 LAT SANDOMIERZA-RATUSZ
ego 12/15
Pamiętnik
CZEKOLAD
ODŻYWIA

# Łańcut Castle

*Magnificent old Łańcut Castle in south east Poland has survived centuries despite the onslaught of foreign armies and buses of kids on school excursions.*

I came here for the first time as a young girl on a scout trip. It was meant to be an educational expedition to show us the unspeakable opulence of Polish aristocracy, as proof of the social inequality of pre-war Poland. Unfortunately that message was lost on us as soon as the baroque palace appeared in the bus driver's windscreen. It was a fairyland, we longed to explore.

LEFT Old ceramic heater in the Corner Salon, Łańcut Castle. ABOVE Łańcut's tiny opera theatre with an 18th-century stage set for Mozart's opera *The Magic Flute*.

In no time all the girls were acting out being princesses, flapping imaginary fans, spinning round and round in fantasy dresses across the grand ballroom's parquet floor. The boys 'drove' coaches in the carriage room, cracking imaginary whips and pulling reins on invisible horses. The teachers watched us play, leaving the history lessons for later. Perhaps, we would listen when the proletarian architecture of our city restored our senses.

After 40 years I still feel like dancing in the ballroom. I still admire Princess Izabela Lubomirska, the 18th-century beauty who turned an old castle into a grand palace, and hosted princes and artists from across Europe. She was renowned for her finesse, blue dresses, and immense wealth. Her ghost is rumoured to haunt the castle. A bluish apparition has been reported drifting through the Great Dining Room, to the Green Salon,

Library, and Sculpture Gallery. She is said to dance in her ballroom, switch around the chairs in the opera theatre, and re-organize, loudly, the brass pots on the pantry shelves.

We stay the night in the cosy hotel inside the castle. We seem to be the only guests. As the temperature drops and a howling wind rattles our shutters, we are sure Izabela is out there, swirling around her wintry park. We urge her to go back to the Corner Salon where she can keep warm next to the beautiful ceramic heater (piec), while we hide deeper under the blankets.

It's a week before Christmas, and the next morning we awake to find Łańcut Castle covered in snow.

RIGHT The Ballroom, Łańcut Castle. OPPOSITE Portrait of Izabela Lubomirska by Marcello Bacciarelli, 1770.

FOLLOWING PAGES Łańcut's Baroque synagogue, 1761, saved from destruction in 1945 by the owner of the castle Alfred Potocki and later protected as a monument by the Polish doctor Władysław Balicki.

ישראל
אי הבל
אחיך
ימחל יסלח ויכפר

הכון לקראת
ותקח מפריו ותאכל

*My grandmother made this only for special occasions, as it contained her rarest and most precious ingredient – sugared orange peel. When I make it today I celebrate the memory of my grandmother and treat the orange peel with the respect it is due, despite its abundance.*

**SERNIK**

# Polish Cheesecake

SERVES 6–8

FOR THE PASTRY (PIE SHELL)
150 g (5 oz) plain (all-purpose) flour
100 g (4 oz) butter
50 g (2 oz) sugar
1 egg yolk
1 tablespoon sour cream

FOR THE FILLING
5 eggs, separated
500g (1lb 2 oz) 'Farm' cheese
200 g (7 oz) caster (superfine) sugar
140 g (4½ oz) butter
1 teaspoon orange oil or essence
50 g (2 oz) potato flour
200 g (7 oz) sultanas (golden raisins)
6 pieces sugared orange peel (see page 33), chopped
icing (powdered) sugar for serving

Knead all the pastry ingredients together with your hands. Form into a ball, wrap in plastic film, and refrigerate for 1 hour.

Grease a 20 cm (8 in) spring-form baking tin. Roll out the pastry about 3 mm (⅛ in) thick. Line the bottom and sides of the baking tin with the pastry. Reserve a small amount for decorating the top of the cheesecake.

To make the filling, beat the egg yolks with the caster (superfine) sugar and softened butter. Break up and soften the cheese well with a fork, then stir it in to the mixture. Add the potato flour add orange oil or essence to taste.

Beat the egg whites until stiff and fold them in. Add the sultanas (golden raisins) and chopped orange peel. Pour the mixture into the pastry case (pie shell).

Preheat the oven to 180°C (350°F). Roll out the reserved ball of pastry about 3 mm (⅛ in) thick and cut into thin strips. Lay these across the top of the cheesecake in a lattice like pattern.

Mix an egg yolk with a little water and glaze the pastry strips before baking for 50 minutes. Allow to cool and leave overnight in the fridge.

Before serving the next day, remove from the cake tin and dust lightly with icing sugar.

# *First Snow*

*My mother woke me when it was still dark. It was only 6am, two hours before school started. She urged me to abandon my thick feather duvet and look out the window. I pressed my face against the cold glass and looked down. And there it was — a pristine white carpet of snow covering roads and footpaths, glistening under sleepy streetlights, awaiting the first rays of sun to test its resilience.*

I ran excitedly between the back and front windows of our apartment, checking that the first snow of winter really had descended. I noticed that our first-floor neighbour, who had a pile of coal delivered by horse and cart earlier that week, had not yet shovelled it into his cellar, so now there was a snow-covered mountain in our backyard. My friends and I would conquer this peak soon after school, ignoring the avalanche of falling coal and black stains on our hands and knees.

I dressed quickly, ready to leave for school early. I hoped the old caretaker could not find his shovel and there would be plenty of snow on the playground to build a snowman before the first bell. Our classes that day seemed to drag forever. Everyone ignored the blackboard, as all heads were turned towards the window, where our coal eyed, pencil nosed snowman was waiting.

OPPOSITE Beata and her mother Lidia, Jelenia Góra, 1964.
ABOVE 1960s Polish matchbox.

Walking home from school, we slid on our shoes, compressing the snow into slippery paths (ślizgawki). We slid again and again, further and further each time, only our school backpacks preventing us from reaching the speed of light. That evening from our third floor apartment, I watched a vast silvery web of these icy tracks shine in the hazy yellow streetlights. They were probably visible from space, and smiling Yuri Gagarin could see them as he orbited the Earth in his spaceship. I waved to him, just in case he could see me, from Vostok 1. Tomorrow, our ślizgawki would be sprinkled with salt and sand, so adults could walk with dignity again, rather than hopping from side to side like children.

ABOVE LEFT Postcard of Karkonosze Mountains in winter.

ABOVE RIGHT Pioneer Russian astronaut Yuri Gagarin.

ADVENT

*Four Sundays before Christmas, my great-grandmother Julia walked to a special pre-dawn mass, 'Roraty,' that marked the start of Advent. In darkness the villagers gathered in a freezing cold church, lit their candles and chanted the prayer Rorate coeli de super...*

*Four Sundays before Christmas, my great-grandmother Julia walked to a special pre-dawn mass, 'Roraty,' that marked the start of Advent. In darkness the villagers gathered in a freezing cold church, lit their candles and chanted the prayer Rorate coeli de super...*

Their hearts and candles burned strongly, until jealous sunrays finally shone through stained glass windows, erasing kneeling shadows from grey stony walls. One special Advent candle wrapped in a white ribbon was left flickering in the daylight as a vigil until Jesus' birth. At home the atmosphere was less solemn: there was St Barbara's Day (Barbórka) and St Nicholas' Day (Święty Mikołaj) to prepare for. For Barbórka I made a black paper hat decorated with colourful feathers – an imitation of the hats miners wore in honour of their patron saint.

SANTA BARBARA
ESPORTATORI

Choinka 1965 r.

# St Nicholas' Day

*I loved the start of December as a child. Long, grey November days were finally over and St Nicholas' Day, on the 6th of December meant Christmas was now not so far off.*

For some time notices had appeared in schools, factories, and kindergartens announcing St Nicholas' arrival at parties for the kids. In the Christian tradition, St Nicholas is the patron saint of children, known for his generosity towards the good and well behaved. In Poland our Santa Claus made an appearance on St Nicholas' Day, as well as on Christmas Eve.

I wrote many pleading letters to St Nicholas with my list of most-desired objects in the world, which in order of importance were 1. Bike, 2. Skates, 3. Beachball, 4. Lollies, 5. No new violin. I handed a sealed envelope, addressed to Santa Claus, to my mother to post, and as luck would have it many of my wishes materialized on the 6th of December. Some of the gifts would arrive late, on Christmas Eve, due to heavy polar storms.

I have no idea how a Catholic saint slipped into the communist calendar. Somehow the brave St Nicholas managed to slide down high factory chimneys and deep mine shafts to reward workers' children with lollies and toys for their good behaviour. He could also give you a bunch of silver twigs instead, but he seemed very forgiving.

ABOVE *Rózga* - sticks to symbolise punishment for naughty children.

LEFT Beata, aged 4, with Santa Claus on St Nicholas Day.

BAŚNIE
NARODÓW
ZWIĄZKU RADZIECKIEGO

*Lollipops are the perfect sweets for a St Nicholas gift bag. This recipe for homemade lollipops uses natural colour and fresh or dried fruit. Lollipops made with dried fruit or mint can last for many days (if you hide them) but any made with fresh fruit will tend to melt after a day.*

## LIZAKI

# *Lollipops*

MAKES 20 MEDIUM LOLLIPOPS

- 20 lollipop sticks
- 450 g (1 lb) caster (superfine) sugar
- 160 ml (⅔ cup) water
- ¼ teaspoon cream of tartar
- oil or non-stick baking spray
- fine slices of orange, lime, fresh or dried strawberries, mint leaves
- various natural food colourings

Spray a baking tray with oil. Lay out your lolly sticks in a line (you can buy these pre made or make your own from wooden kebab skewers).

Push slices of your favourite fruits, such as lemon or lime, or dried strawberry pieces or mint leaves, onto the ends of the sticks.

Melt the sugar with the water and cream of tartar in a heavy-bottomed saucepan. Heat at a high temperature for at least 10 minutes until the syrup becomes thick and a pale honey colour.

Remove the pan from the heat and immediately place it in a bowl of ice to stop the syrup from cooking any further.

To make different coloured lollipops, divide sugar mixture into separate cups for colouring, and and mix in a few drops of your chosen food colouring. Pour a small amount on to the end of each stick, coating the fruit. Quickly repeat with the rest of the syrup and different colours for different fruits.

In a few minutes the lollipops will set solid and can be gently lifted off the tray.

# Mama Druga's Christmas

*Every year my family gathered for Christmas at my grandmother's house.*

Preparations started weeks ahead, as jars of beetroots, cabbage, and mushrooms made their way from the dark, cold cellar up into her warm kitchen. Like treasures from a sunken ship, they were inspected in the sharp light of the lamp for their content and worth. All the fruits and vegetables, carefully preserved in summer, were now tasted with the tiniest of teaspoons and hopefully accepted for the upcoming Christmas feast.

When the cooking finally started, I watched the show from my corner of the old oak table, the best seat in the house. The kitchen, like an orchestra, was tuning for its greatest concert of the year. Kettles whistled high C, pestles drummed, pots and pans "percussed" with gusto, only to be hushed by a shower of poppy seeds falling into an enamel pot.

Daring tongues of golden flames from the wood fire escaped from the white-tiled stove and greedily licked heavy copper pots of beetroot soup. My grandmother was the conductor, bowing with a smile to her 5-year-old adoring granddaughter. It was still some days until the family would gather, for the most sacred evening of all – Christmas Eve.

*Pierogi – ravioli-like pasta dumplings – are perhaps the most popular item on the Polish menu. Pierogi with cabbage and mushrooms is the traditional dish for Christmas Eve, when no meat can be served.*

PIEROGI Z KAPUSTĄ I GRZYBAMI

# *Pierogi with Cabbage and Mushrooms*

MAKES ABOUT 100 pierogi

FOR THE PASTA DOUGH
- 125 g (4½ oz) unsalted butter
- 1 kg (2 lb 3 oz) plain (all-purpose) flour
- 0.5 l (about 1 pint) warm water
- extra butter for frying onion

FOR THE FILLING
- 6–8 dried porcini mushrooms
- 2 kg (4 lb 6 oz) jar sauerkraut (pickled cabbage)
- 2 onions
- 50 g (2 oz) butter
- salt and pepper
- extra onion for decoration

Soak dried mushrooms for an hour, then bring to the boil with a pinch of salt and simmer gently for 15 minutes. Drain and set aside.

Soften the butter, then slowly work it with your fingers into the flour on a large wooden board. Add the warm water, little by little, to make an elastic, soft pastry dough.

Flour the board, then roll out to about 3 mm (⅛ in) thickness. Use an inverted tumbler to cut out pastry circles about 7 cm (3 in) in diameter.

Rinse and drain the sauerkraut. Place in a large saucepan, cover with water, and bring to the boil. Simmer for a couple of minutes then drain and squeeze out water with a muslin cloth (cheesecloth). When dry, chop the cabbage finely.

Chop the onion and fry in 2 teaspoons of butter. Add the cabbage and fry together on a medium heat for 5 minutes. Add the mushrooms, chopped into 5 mm (¼ in) slices. Season with salt and pepper.

Allow to cool before placing a teaspoonful of filling on each circle of pastry. Seal the pierogi by folding the circle in half and crimping edges together with your fingers.

Bring a large saucepan of salted water to the boil and add the pierogi, stirring carefully to prevent them sticking together. The pierogi will float to the top as soon as they are cooked, which only takes a minute or so. Remove and drain well in a strainer before serving with melted butter and more fried onion.

*My grandmother Józefa served me prune kompot in an intricately decorated antique crystal glass. This chocolate coloured drink was made especially for Christmas but I was allowed to taste it a few days before.*

## KOMPOT Z SUSZONYCH ŚLIWEK

# Prune Fruit Drink

MAKES 6 LARGE GLASSES

200 g (c. 7 oz) prunes
1.5 l (6 cups) water
50 g (2 oz) caster (superfine) sugar
1 teaspoon ground cloves
1 teaspoon ground cinnamon or 1 cinnamon stick
honey and sugar to decorate the glasses

Put the prunes, water, sugar, cloves, and cinnamon in a large saucepan and bring to the boil. Simmer gently for 1 hour. Strain the liquid into a jug. Serve warm.

Decorate Christmas glasses by dipping a finger in some honey, then running it around the rims of the glasses. Invert the glasses and dip them in a saucer full of sugar to coat the rims with a sugary frosting.

Prunes strained from the drink are a delicious dessert on their own.

AROUND THE WORLD WITH BOLEK &
Wielka podròż BOLKA i LOLKA

Naklad 1.844.00
Przy
NR22(115)

# Kraków

*Colourful miniature models of the Mariacki Church and nativity scenes – called szopki – are displayed in Kraków's main square in early December. Competition entries come from as far as Chicago, where Polish customs are never forgotten.*

As a child I made szopki too. I used colourful scrap wrapping paper, piled up in layers on my grandmother's kitchen table to craft the tall towers of St Mary's. Glued to a cardboard floor they invariably leaned to one side, and had to be supported by buttresses of wooden twigs brought in from the garden. Baby Jesus, made of plastelina (Polish "Play-Doh"), lay in a matchbox manger, filled with real hay. He smiled at his mother with thickly rolled red lips as she knelt at his feet. Her celestial blue robe, always made from the freshest, never-before-used plastelina, billowed about her in waves. Cows and sheep, made from older plastelina with the colours fused together, stared at giant-petalled flowers sprouting from the ground. I made a Bethlehem star from the gold foil around a chocolate bar that still bore flakes of chocolate, and hung it on a thread between the church towers to twinkle joyously and stop baby Jesus crying. It was unnecessary, of course, as he was always happy and warm, just as I was in my grandmother's kitchen.

LEFT St Mary's Church, Kraków, with szopki on display. ABOVE Lajkonik - a symbol of Kraków

FOLLOWING PAGES Christmas markets, Kraków Old Town Square.

DA PIETRO

# Chanukah

*"Chanukah, oh Chanukah"... we join in the singing at the Jewish Community Centre in Kraków. Christmas time is Chanukah time for Polish Jews. I watch Jewish kids laughing with Poland's chief rabbi, who like St Nicholas hands out sweets.*

On Friday night we share chałka bread at a special Sabbath Chanukah dinner, just as I shall share a bread wafer with my family on Christmas Eve. Our traditions are so similar, since Poland was home to so many Jews for centuries. I am welcomed into my Jewish friends' home and the sweet smell of chałka was the same in my grandmother's kitchen.

I feel moved when I hold my Jewish friends' hands. Salty tears scratch my throat during murmured prayers to the old almighty God, the creator of this mysterious and inexplicable universe. Maybe it is just the salt on the chałka bread and I must wash it down with a shot of Polish vodka. "Chanukah, oh Chanukah..."

*Challah (chałka) is a traditional Jewish bread baked for Shabbath. It is also popular in Polish bakeries, usually served for breakfast with butter and jam. This is my friend Connie's recipe, which uses 4 strands of dough plaited together (3 is easier but not as pretty).*

CHAŁKA

# Connie's Challah Bread

MAKES 2 MEDIUM LOAVES

- 14 g (2 × 7 g or ¼ oz packets) dried yeast
- 300 ml (c. 1¼ cups) hand-hot water
- 50 g (2 oz) caster (superfine) sugar
- 60 ml (¼ cup) vegetable oil
- 1 teaspoon salt
- 1 egg + 1 extra for glazing
- 600 g (1 lb 5 oz) plain (all-purpose) flour
- sesame or poppy seeds to decorate

In a large mixing bowl, dissolve the yeast in 120 ml (½ cup) of warm water. Add the sugar, oil, salt, and 1 egg and mix together well. Then add the remaining water.

Slowly stir in the flour and mix into a soft dough. Turn out onto a floured board and knead well for 5 minutes. Shape into a large ball, cover with a clean cloth, and leave in a warm place for a couple of hours to double in size. Connie often leaves her dough overnight, then bakes it the following morning.

To shape the bread, divide the dough into 2 balls. Put 1 aside and cover with a clean cloth until you are ready to work with it and divide the other into 4 smaller balls. Shape each ball into long strands. It is easiest to make the strands in stages – first taking each ball to 15 cm (6 in), then 22 cm (9 in), and then to the full 30 cm (12 in) length. Somehow the dough seems to enjoy the rest between each stage.

To plait 4 strands, pinch them all together at one end, then spread them out to form a double V-shape on your wooden board. Now thread the strands right over left for the pair on the right, and right over left for the pair on the left. Then for the pair in the middle take the left strand over the right one. Repeat this sequence until you reach the ends of the strands, then pinch them all together and tuck the join neatly under the end of the loaf.

Lightly beat the second egg with a little water and glaze both loaves. Sprinkle poppy or sesame seeds on top if you wish to decorate the bread.

Place in a cold oven and then heat the oven to 220°C (425°F). Bake for 30 minutes, checking from time to time. The loaves are done when they are nicely browned on top and give off a hollow sound when tapped on the bottom. Leave to cool on a wire rack.

# *Wieliczka Salt Mine*

*Most Polish kids who attended schools in the 1960s, 70s and 80s remember a compulsory school excursion to the Wieliczka Salt Mine on the edge of Kraków. Who could forget descending 378 steps, spiralling down a wooden staircase and getting giddy at the bottom, and... licking the salty walls when the teacher wasnt looking.*

We walked for hours, holding hands, along poorly lit, low-roofed corridors that joined various chambers, staircases, and chapels. Jumping out of dark corners, the boys scared the girls, who screamed with delight in response. Such was the script to be followed in all Primary School educational trips. We were fascinated by the legend of Princess Kinga's ring, lost in a Hungarian mine hundred of miles away, then found here, deep under the town of Wieliczka where it was jealously guarded by the earth's salty rocks and by Skarbnik, the mine's legendary ghost.

ABOVE Statue of Princess Kinga, carved out of rock salt. LEFT Underground chamber, several storeys high.

FOLLOWING PAGES Christmas nativity scene carved from rock salt by Mieczysław Kluzek, 1970s.

Today the mine is well lit and friendly guides allow you to lick the walls – so you don't. Your first glimpse at the vast St Kinga's Chapel is still breathtaking. A silver coloured underground cathedral, with chandeliers and sculptures, is entirely carved from rock salt. All this extraordinary art, deep down below the earth's surface, feels like divine creation. Perhaps Holy Mary's sorrowful tears fell from her altar and sculpted the cathedral's salty walls in memory of her son.

# Christmas Carol

You did not know, Holy Mary
Where to lay the fruit of your birth
A cradle from hay you made
Like no-one had on earth

A cradle laid with hay
In a stable where baby's room stands
A pillow made for your son
With gentle, motherly hands

You held in your arms your child
And sang lullaby baby
And throughout silent night resounds
The voice of our holiest lady

Ela Chylewska, 1992
(trans. Natalia O'Keefe)

# Kolęda

*Nie wiedziałaś Matko Najświętsza*
*na czym położyć swe dziecię*
*wyścieliłaś sianem kołyskę*
*jakiej nikt nie miał na świecie*

*Wyścieliłaś kołyskę sianem*
*mały żłobek w pustej stajence*
*położyłaś synkowi pod głowę*
*poduszeczkę – matczyne ręce*

*I tuliłaś w dłoniach swe dziecię*
*i śpiewałaś mu luli, luli*
*a wśród nocnej ciszy rozbrzmiewał*
*głos radosny Najświętszej Matuli.*

RADIO W

*There is no longer journey than that made on Christmas Eve as you try to get home in time for dinner. We have been travelling around Poland for weeks, but today we must reach my village before that special first star appears.*

*There is no longer journey than that made on Christmas Eve as you try to get home in time for dinner. We have been travelling around Poland for weeks, but today we must reach my village before that special first star appears.*

ZDYM DOMU
PZ BYSTRZYCA PRZEC. 64 ZAP. 25 GR

I can already smell Aunt Sabina's beetroot barszcz though we have hundreds of kilometres still to drive. I cannot wait to see Mama Druga's house again, hug the linden tree outside, and dabble my fingers in the garden stream. We started out at dawn, with no stopping for petrol, coffee, or photography allowed. Simon begs me to stop fiddling with the radio: "Why not tell me about... Christmas? Christmas in your grandmother's house." It isn't a hard task, my memories from more than 40 years ago are still so vivid. I talk and talk, as he drives and drives...

# Expedition to the Attic

*Each year, a few days before Christmas Eve, I was allowed to make a thrilling expedition to the attic in search of our precious Christmas decorations. My grandmother gave me a rectangular metal torch that had colourful plastic filters which you could switch around to change the light from yellow to green to red. Technology could not get better than that.*

I climbed the steep and squeaky stairs, followed closely by the cat, who was always ready to inspect our roof from the inside. I opened the heavy trapdoor, minding my head, and shone my torch through lacy frozen spider webs and onto frost-crocheted patterns on the attic window. The slimmest ray of winter sun cast a beam from the window to the dusty, wooden floor, as if to indicate where the golden pot was buried.

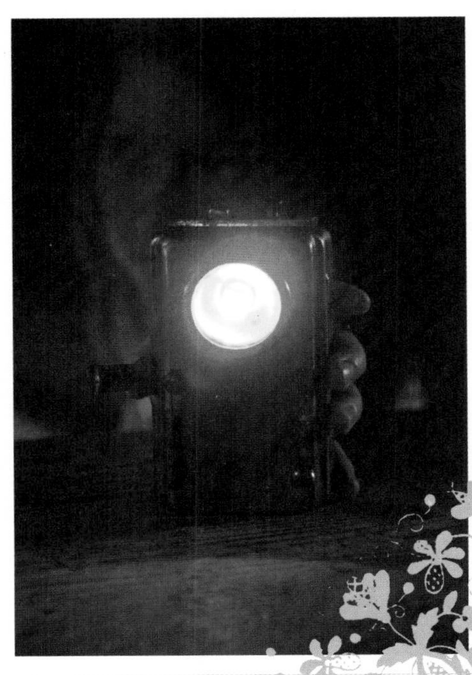

There were many treasures... the old, worn suitcases that had travelled here on a one way train ticket from Lwów in 1945. Behind them, my great-grandfather Dimitri's carpenter's box, which though banned from use by the communist government in 1948 still contained shiny and sharp tools, ready for making more barrels for sour cabbage and cucumbers. A stack of Girlfriend (*Przyjaciółka*) the women's newspaper saved by Julia from the flames of the kitchen stove, were gathered in a yellowing cardboard box. The cover girl on the top of the pile smiled at me, her face freckled by poppy seeds fallen from husks hung to dry above.

I knew exactly where the decorations were kept, but I couldn't resist snooping around, shining my torch into dark and mysterious corners, burrowing into boxes to discover my family's secrets inside. I stayed in the attic as long as I could, until my grandmother's voice urged me to return to the kitchen. She wooed me down with freshly made poppy-seed noodles. And for the cat, there were fish heads, staring up at the attic from a bowl on the floor below.

Nakład 1.844.000 egz.
Przyjaciółka
NR 22 (115)
TYGODNIK

ZUPA GRATIS!
SZKOLNA

*Poppy seed pancakes are traditional Christmas fare in many parts of Poland. This recipe comes from the city of Elbląg.*

NALEŚNIKI Z MAKIEM

# *Poppy-seed Pancakes with Orange*

MAKES 8 PANCAKES

FOR THE POPPY-SEED FILLING

- 200 g (7 oz) poppy seed
- 600 ml (2½ cups) milk
- 50 g (2 oz) sultanas (golden raisins)
- zest of 1 small orange
- finely chopped peel of 1 small orange
- 150 g (5 oz) caster (superfine) sugar
- 120 ml (½ cup) water
- 5 tablespoons honey
- orange oil or essence, if desired

FOR THE PANCAKES

- 300 g (11 oz) self-raising flour
- 350 ml (1½ cups) milk
- 50 g (2 oz) caster (superfine) sugar
- 3 eggs
- 120 ml (½ cup) water
- 50 g (2 oz) unsalted butter for frying

Simmer poppy seed in milk gently for 10 minutes, then leave to soak for about 12 hours. Drain and put through a grinder so poppy seeds become a paste.

Add pre-softened sultanas (golden raisins). They can be softened by soaking in water for 2 hours or simmered for 10 minutes.

Simmer the orange zest and peel for 5 minutes in a saucepan with 1 tablespoon of sugar and 120 ml (½ cup) of water.

Warm the honey to make it easier to pour, then add to the poppy-seed paste with the rest of the sugar and the orange peel mix. Stir together well. For a stronger orange flavour add a few drops of orange oil or essence to taste.

To make the pancakes, combine the flour, milk, sugar, pinch of salt, and water. Beat the eggs and whisk in. Refrigerate for half an hour to make the batter smoother.

Melt a knob of butter in a hot frying pan (skillet) and add a dollop of the batter mix to form a pancake. The pan needs to be really hot so the batter cooks quite quickly. Cook for a minute then flip over and cook the other side.

Spread the poppy-seed filling on the pancake. Roll it up and serve.

*There can never be too many poppy seed dishes to serve on Christmas Eve. I love them all. My grandmother made pasta stars and mixed them with poppy seeds, sultanas and nuts.*

KLUSKI Z MAKIEM

# *Poppy-seed Pasta*

SERVES 4

200 g (7 oz) poppy seeds
600 ml (2 ½ cups) milk
4 tablespoons honey
100 g (4 oz) sultanas (golden raisins)
50 g (2 oz) chopped almonds
1 tablespoon sugared orange peel, chopped (see page 32)
500 g (1 lb 2 oz) cooked egg pasta
25 g (1 oz) unsalted butter if desired

Put the poppy seeds in a large saucepan and add the milk. Bring to the boil, stirring. Simmer for 10 minutes, then leave to soak overnight.

The next day, drain the poppy seeds and grind them to a paste.

Put the paste in a saucepan on a low heat and mix in the honey, sultanas (golden raisins), almonds, and sugared orange peel.

Stir the butter through the cooked pasta then add the poppy-seed paste and mix well. Serve hot or cold.

CHROŃ MAK
PRZED SZKODNIKAMI
RSOPUL

# Decorating the Tree

*Sparkling stars, animals, clowns, angels, and Santa Clauses... forgotten and fragile old friends smiled and spun with joy on long dusty threads when I pulled them up from their beds of straw in cardboard boxes.*

My job was to hang the delicate decorations on a freshly cut pine tree, still fragrant with amber sap. I was always careful to leave plenty of room below the bottom branches for any large parcels that Santa Claus might be bringing on Christmas Eve.

For weeks before Christmas I had been making metres of coloured paper chains. Now I had to wrap the tree in a continuous spiral. No breaks were acceptable, and if any links fell apart they had to be re-glued, even if the chain was already hanging on the tree. The soggy paper tasted of mouldy apples as I licked and licked, desperate to make it stick. After all, no matter how revolting the glue, this chain represented the togetherness of my family and had to hold strong. The best way to get rid of the taste was to lick the sweet candy canes that also hung on the tree. Unfortunately that meant that by Christmas many of the coloured foil wrappers contained wooden pencils, instead of candy canes.

OPPOSITE Christmas trees for sale outside St Mary's Church, Kraków.

I could decorate the lower branches on my own. To place the large crystal star at the top of the Christmas tree I needed my father to lift me high in the air. We made multiple attempts, nearly pulling the whole tree down, before I managed to lodge it right at the peak. I was applauded loudly by Józefa and smiled at by Julia, who looked up from her book for a moment, only to return to her reading, stroking the cat on her lap. The cat gazed at me sleepily, never impressed by my tree climbing efforts.

It is an old Slavic tradition to hang a Christmas tree upside down. The podłaźniczka is hung from the ceiling and dressed in walnuts, paper chains, apples, and gingerbreads. It wasn't until the late 18th century that our German neighbours stood it upright in their dining rooms. We found a Christmas tree set the correct way, upside down, inside Warsaw's Ethnographic Museum.

# The First Star

*My grandmother Józefa draped a crisp, white cloth over the old kitchen table around midday each Christmas Eve. This was her happy announcement that the cooking had come to an end.*

After mercilessly enduring days of clattering chopping knives, rolling pins, and crushing grinders the table was finally allowed to sleep for a few hours. My grandmother was ready in her best flowery dress squashed under a freshly starched, disciplined apron. She stood next to the hot stove, which Julia had fed that morning with chips of pine wood and a millefeuille of copies of Gazeta Robotnicza, the communist workers' newspaper that burnt with a revolutionary zest and passion for destruction.

Józefa inspected her pots, adjusting their lids, allowing narrow impatient streams of vapour to escape to the cold ceiling only to return in heavy droplets on to a hissing hot plate. The lids vibrated with excitement like tiny bells on three-horse sleighs. An army of mushroom dumplings stood by under tea towel tents, ready to jump into hot water minutes before the first guests arrived.

"Two Girls" by Olga Boznańska, 1896.

It was a non-negotiable tradition that Christmas Eve dinner could only start with the appearance of the first evening star. Glued to the kitchen window, I watched the linen-white winter sky intensely all afternoon, eager for the celebrations to begin. Different lights appeared but then disappeared, as if teaching me to be patient. Shining dragons, silver fairies, and lost Russian sputniks traversed my patrolled horizon. My breath fogged the glass that stopped me from reaching out and touching the sky with my finger.

When my family finally arrived after work on the day's last bus from the city, I could not abandon my observation post, but jumped and waved to them enthusiastically. Soon I could hear them in the hall downstairs, laughing and talking over each other, stamping the snow off their heavy boots. I knew they had changed into more elegant shoes, when I heard the staccato of high heels on the old oak corridor floors. One by one my mother, my father, my aunt, and my uncle appeared in the kitchen doorway in their best evening wear, straightening their beads and tightening their ties, ready for great-grandmother Julia's silent inspection.

They kissed and hugged Julia and Józefa, commentating on the tantalising aromas coming from the stove.
My father picked me up and tossed me in the air, making me giggle and scream, but ruining my French curls and carefully tied white chiffon ribbons. I quickly returned to my post, hoping not to have missed that elusive Christmas star. After many false alarms one shy light would finally become fixed to the darkening sky. Dragged to the window for the hundredth time, Julia pronounced that the Bethlehem star had indeed appeared and we could all at last sit down to eat.

OPPOSITE "Hope" by Kazimierz Wojniakowski, 1807.

# *Wigilia*

*My family, like many others, gathered together every 24th December for a special meal, called Wigilia. On that most sacred night of the year, we shared food, stories and songs, while waiting for baby Jesus to be born.*

My great grandmother Julia, like a high priestess, stood at the top of the table. Her waist-long silver hair was plaited into a bun on the back of her head, held in place with sharp hairpins. Her black, straight woollen dress emphasized her tall upright body that refused to bow to the grief of widowhood and loneliness. She held the opłatek wafer in her left hand, while her right crossed her heart. She whispered a blessing from a prayer book that had survived two world wars, and was as old and dignified as she was. Then we shared the opłatek between us with great reverence, wishing each other health and happiness in the approaching year. I let my wafer slowly melt on my tongue, enjoying the tingling sensation. I was certain it had magic powers, and if I swallowed it with a solemn expression, all my Christmas wishes would come true.

ABOVE 'Staś sleeping' by Stanisław Wyspiański, 1904

OPPOSITE Opłatek is the wafer purchased from church, broken, then shared with everyone at the Christmas table, with a hug and a kiss. INSET "The Black Madonna" from Holy Trinity Church, Tykocin.

Our dinner always started with red barszcz. Firstly, wild mushroom dumplings were placed on the bottom of each soup bowl. This was the time to grab one and swallow it quickly then complain with a straight face about being given one fewer than everyone else. Another dumpling was then dutifully handed out by Mama Druga so all was fair at her table. Hot ruby-coloured barszcz was then poured over the mushroom dumplings turning the pastry pink. It tasted divine, every mouthful lifted ceremoniously in a large silver spoon.

We could have eaten several bowlfuls but we knew that the next dish was already waiting. Now it was the turn of pierogi with cabbage and mushrooms to arrive, and the competition would start again, with new records set for numbers of pierogi eaten at one sitting.

Carp in aspic followed, then cabbage and peas, poppyseed noodles, cheesecakes, ginger bread, and my favourite desert of all – kutia. I drank kompot from large crystal glasses and chewed on soft, cinnamon-spiced prunes. My family seemed to be getting on fabulously, finishing Julia's bottles of homemade liqueur – nalewki.

As the evening wore on I liked to curl up on a little green-velvet sofa in the corner of the dining room. I promised myself that I would not fall asleep, but year after year failed miserably, and missed out on seeing Santa Claus arriving to place boxes and gifts under the Christmas tree. I always awoke, pretending I had never been asleep, when my father came to move me to my bed. I would break free and run towards the Christmas tree to unwrap my long-awaited treasures.

*Fresh fish in winter was a true delicacy. One or two small fresh water carp had to feed the whole family. My grandmother skilfully transformed the fish into colourful jelly domes, full of vegetables and white speckles of fish.*

## Karp w galarecie

# *Carp in Aspic*

SERVES 6

- 1 whole carp (or any white fish)
- 6 medium-sized onions, chopped finely
- 6 peeled carrots (3 sliced and 3 left whole)
- ½ bunch parsley
- 1 tablespoon caster (superfine) sugar
- 2 cubes fish or chicken stock (bouillon)
- 2 × 10 g (½ oz) packets gelatin

Clean, scale, and gut the fish and place it in a fish poacher or large saucepan. Cover with water. Add all the carrots and the onions. Bring to the boil and simmer gently for 20 minutes.

Remove the fish and the whole carrots, putting them aside for later. Allow the fish to cool, then remove the white flesh from the bones and skin using your fingers, breaking it into small pieces. Put the remaining bones, head, and fish skin back into the pot with the crumbled stock (bouillon) cubes and sugar. Simmer for another 60 minutes to create the stock.

Strain the fish stock through a muslin cloth (cheesecloth) and allow the liquid to cool a little. Add salt and pepper to taste. Dissolve the gelatin in 0.5 l (2 cups) of liquid, then stir back into the stock.

Finely chop the parsley and thinly slice the whole carrots. Divide the parsley, carrots, and fish pieces between six small ramekins or moulds, leaving some room for the stock which will form the jelly around the ingredients. Fill the ramekins with the strained stock right to their rims so they have a flat surface. Refrigerate for about 4 hours, or until the jelly has set firmly.

Turn out the ramekins onto plates, warming the moulds if necessary by dipping them in hot water to loosen the jelly inside. Serve with fresh bread. (Vodka shot traditional but optional).

*Barszcz is the signature soup many Poles eat on Christmas Eve. This is my Aunt Sabina's version, made from vegetable stock and beetroot, and poured over wild mushroom dumplings.*

## BARSZCZ CZERWONY Z USZKAMI

# Beetroot Soup (with Wild Mushroom dumplings)

Enough for 4

- 2 kg (4 ½ lb) beetroot (beets)
- 3 carrots, chopped
- 1 onion, chopped
- 1 small celeriac, sliced
- 1 stalk celery, sliced
- 1 small bunch parsley, chopped
- 1 bay leaf
- 1 clove garlic, crushed
- 1 teaspoon caster (superfine) sugar
- 2.5 l (c. 4 pints) water
- 1 tablespoon lemon juice or apple vinegar

Add the carrots, onion, celeriac, bay leaf, parsley and celery to a large saucepan with the water. Bring to the boil and simmer until the vegetables are soft.

Peel and grate the beetroot using the largest holes in your grater. Add to the pot and simmer on low heat. After 15 minutes add the lemon juice or apple vinegar. After a further 15 minutes strain and add crushed garlic, salt, pepper and sugar.

Serve very hot with wild mushroom dumplings (uszka – see page 151).

*Dumplings with wild mushrooms served with hot red beetroot barszcz are served as the very first dish on Christmas Eve. They are consumed with such piety that I find it hard to eat them at any other time of the year without feeling disrespectful.*

USZKA Z GRZYBAMI

# *Wild Mushroom Dumplings*

Cover the mushrooms in water, and soak for a few hours. Bring to the boil and simmer for ten minutes. Drain and grind in a food processor.

Dice the onion finely and fry in a little oil over a low heat until translucent. Add the mushrooms and fry for a few minutes. Add salt and pepper.

Mix the flour and butter or oil on a large wooden board with your hands. Add a little warm water to make an elastic dough. Take a tennis-ball-sized lump of dough and roll it out on your floured board to 3 mm (1/8 in) thick. Use a small inverted tumbler or pastry cutter – about 6 cm (2½ in) in diameter – to cut out pastry circles. Repeat until all the pastry has been used.

Place a teaspoonful of the mushroom filling on one half of each circle and fold it over to form a dumpling. Use your thumb and second finger to seal the folded semicircle, pinching all along the rounded edges in a shell-like pattern. Then fold the two outer tips of your dumpling and join them together by pinching. This creates the classic uszka shape ('small ears') like Italian tortellini.

Cook the dumplings in a large saucepan of salted boiling water. This will only take a couple of minutes – they are ready when they float to the top. Remove with a slotted spoon and drain.

Serve 4–5 dumplings or uszka per person in a bowl of hot beetroot (beets) soup (see page 148).

MAKES ENOUGH FOR 6

FOR THE FILLING
150 g (5 oz) dried mushrooms
1 large onion
vegetable oil

FOR THE PASTRY DOUGH
500 g (1 lb 2 oz) plain (all-purpose) flour
50 g (2 oz) butter or 3 tablespoons vegetable oil
warm water

*A traditional vegetarian dish served on Christmas Eve. A true winter recipe, made from split peas kept in cotton bags in the pantry, dried mushrooms hanging in the attic and pickled cabbage from oak barrels stacked in a frosty cellar – while the kitchen garden slept under snow.*

## WIGILIJNA KAPUSTA Z GROCHEM

# *Christmas Eve Cabbage and Split Peas*

SERVES 6

- 250 g (9 oz) yellow split peas
- 1 kg (2¼ lb) jar sauerkraut cabbage
- 1 medium-sized onion
- 25 g (1 oz) butter or 1 tablespoon vegetable oil
- 4–5 dried porcini mushrooms

Soak the peas overnight. Next day, bring to the boil and simmer for 30 minutes. Drain, remove one third of the peas and mash the rest. Simmer mushrooms gently for ten minutes. Put to one side.

Rinse the cabbage then place in a saucepan and cover with water. Bring to the boil and simmer for 45 minutes. Drain.

Chop the onion and fry in the butter or oil for 5–8 minutes until translucent and starting to brown.

Add the cabbage and mashed peas to the onion. Drain and chop the mushrooms, then add to the pan. Fry together on low heat for a few minutes, adding in the un-mashed peas to give the dish some bite. Season to taste.

*Kutia is an old Slavic, pre-Christian dessert. A concoction of poppy seeds, honey, wheat, nuts, and fruit was consumed on the longest night of the year, during a ritual to remember family ancestors. The dish has survived for millenia and has been adopted as part of the Christian Christmas Eve tradition.*

## KUTIA

# *Christmas poppy seed dessert*

SERVES 4

- 240 g (10 oz) poppy seeds
- 600 ml (2½ cups) milk
- 200 g (7 oz) large grain pearl barley (*kasza jęczmienna*)
- 6 tablespoons honey
- 100 g (4 oz) raisins
- 50 g (2 oz) whole almonds. coarsely crushed
- 100 g (4 oz) walnuts
- zest of 1 small lemon
- zest or 1 small orange
- 8 strips of sugared orange peel, chopped (see page 32)

Place the poppy seeds in a saucepan and add the milk, stir, and bring to the boil. Simmer for 15 minutes. Stir frequently so the milk doesn't burn. Cover and leave to soak overnight in the fridge.

Next day stir the soaked poppy seeds, pour out any excess liquid, then grind in a food processor on its finest setting.

Cook the barley in a heavy-bottomed pot according to the instructions on the packet. (We use 3 cups cold water for 1 cup of barley). Bring to the boil then simmer on lowest heat for about 45 minutes, stirring frequently. If the barley starts to dry out as it cooks, top up the water.

Allow to cool.

Chop the nuts together coarsely. Add the nuts, barley and all remaining ingredients to the the poppy-seed paste. Stir together well. Chill in the fridge for a few hours before serving at the end of the Wigilia meal. Any leftovers are delicious eaten for breakfast.

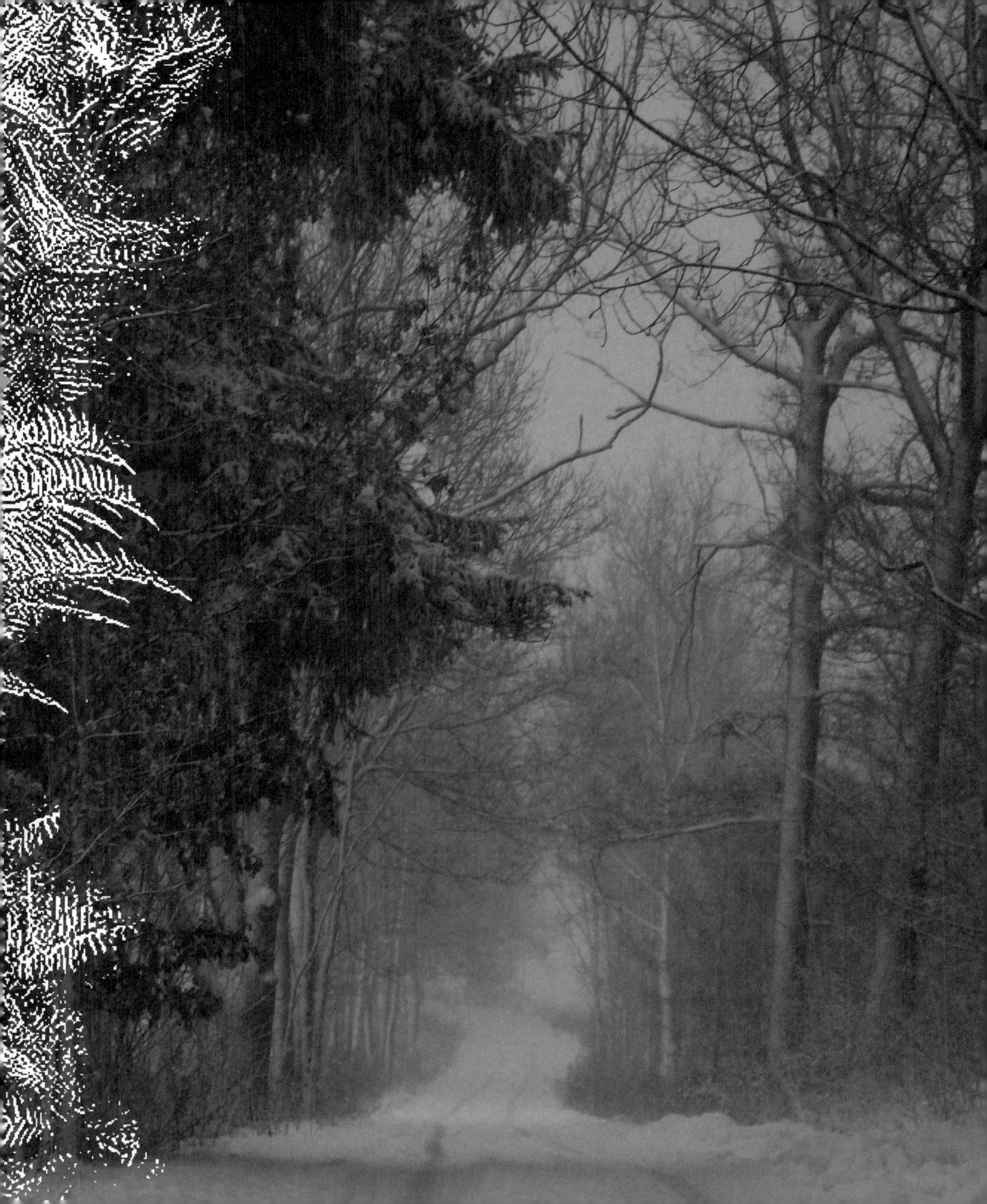

# The Night the Animals Talk

*Christmas Eve culminated in a midnight mass held in the village church. My great grandmother Julia wrapped herself in a long black scarf and headed out into the snow. Fit as a teenager, though in her 80s,*

she ignored the family's pleas to slow down, promising the chance to see the best nativity scene ever built. I stayed in bed, hugging my gifts under thick feather duvets, listening to the noises coming from the village, on the only night of the year when animals could 'talk'.

*Chodzi konik po kolędzie*
*Robić na chleb jeszcze będzie*

*The horse who goes a-carrolling*
*Earns bread money*

The horses were probably chatting about the fun they had walking from house to house, led by noisy and mischievous youths singing carols (kolędy). I tried to listen in case the horses were joining in the old Polish carol: *Chodzi konik po kolędzie*... The cows, I imagined, shared their dreamy stories of green pastures full of clover and dandelions. I was sure that our cat whinged about his 'hard' life on the kitchen sofa, to our neighbour's dog, who lived outside and howled from his kennel.

I gazed out the window at our cherry tree, heavy with snow. It had been lovingly wrapped by Julia in a protective straw tunic to stay warm in a chilly winter. It swayed in the wind, and I heard a whispered promise of buckets of sweet cherries to come in July.

# *Christmas Day*

*From the early hours of Christmas Day I sat at my corner of the kitchen table playing with my gifts and colouring my new books. Mama Druga woke early too, ready to prepare a feast for the special Christmas Breakfast.*

LEFT "A Country Madonna" by Stanisław Wyspiański, 1904.

My family, who had endured the long midnight sermon in church, were allowed to sleep in, except for my great grandmother Julia who was always miraculously the first to rise, dress, and light up the kitchen stove. She sat quietly on the sofa, her body straight and feet together, her face replaced by a large book.

Józefa was making the caraway bread, and I watched fascinated as her fingers became webbed together with elastic strands of dough. I kneaded my own small loaves from a lump of pastry thrown at me with laughter across the table. The aroma of freshly baked bread soon woke my hungry family who was somehow ready to eat again. Everybody zealously denied breaking into the pantry after church the previous night to sample sausages.

Now meat was allowed after the advent fast. Józefa carefully sliced the long spicy sausages, pink juicy ham, veal marinated with onions, and baked paté (pasztet). Our cat's affection for Józefa could not be greater at that moment as his black tail brushed against my grandmother's stockings. He got to taste some ham before anyone else, such was the hierarchy in the household. Breakfast soon stretched into lunch and some of yesterday's cabbage and mushroom pierogi were fried in fresh butter until crisp and golden.

In the afternoon we went for a long walk around the village. My father pulled my sledge with me wrapped in blankets, safely secured by a fat cat stretched across my knees. Groups of boys and girls were walking from house to house carol singing. I could not wait for them to arrive at our door: I knew they would be rewarded for their efforts with sweets and cakes.

OPPOSITE Old Polish Christmas cards. 'Wesołych Świąt' means 'Merry Christmas.'

WYJĄTKOWYCH ŚWIĄT
Piernikarnia Toruńska

Wesołych Świąt!

WESOŁYCH ŚWIĄT!
Na pasterkę

Wesołych Świąt!

*The smell of freshly baked caraway bread always reminds me of Christmas morning. It takes me back to my grandmother's warm kitchen and straight into her loving arms.*

CHLEB Z KMINKIEM

# Caraway Rye Bread

MAKES 2 MEDIUM LOAVES

- 14 g (2 × 7g or ¼ oz packets) dried active yeast
- 0.5 l (2 cups) warm water
- 2 tablespoons caraway seeds
- 2 teaspoons salt
- 1 tablespoon vegetable oil
- 2 tablespoons dark brown sugar
- 375 g (13 oz) rye flour
- 450 g (1 lb) wholemeal plain (whole wheat all-purpose) flour

Dissolve the yeast in 120 ml (½ cup) water in a large mixing bowl.

Add the caraway seeds, salt, oil, brown sugar and the rest of the water. Mix together well and slowly stir in the rye flour. Add about half of the wholemeal (whole wheat) flour and mix until smooth. Then add enough of the remaining flour to make a soft, elastic dough.

Knead on a floured board for 10 minutes. Cover and leave in a warm place for about 1 hour to double in size.

Punch (knock) down the dough and divide into two. Shape the dough into 2 narrow loaf tins 23 × 13 × 7 cm (9 × 5 × 3 in). Cover and leave for another 30 minutes for the loaves to rise again.

Meanwhile pre-heat the oven to 190°C (375°F).

Bake the loaves for 30 minutes until they are firm and brown on the top.

*This Christmas paté is for true meat lovers. It is a smooth mixture of pork, beef and chicken. It tastes divine after long days of advent when no meat is allowed.*

## Pasztet

# *Baked Paté*

MAKES 2 MEDIUM MEATLOAVES

- 500 g (1 lb 6 oz) pork neck
- 500 g (1 lb 6 oz) beef ribs
- 500 g (1 lb 6 oz) chicken "merrylands" – chicken thigh and drumstick together
- 60 g (2½ oz) chicken livers
- 2 medium-sized onions
- 6 peppercorns
- 1 bay leaf
- 1 cup milk
- 6 whole allspice, crushed
- 3 egg whites
- 3 egg yolks
- 4 tbs olive oil
- 2 small white bread rolls (stale)

Roughly chop the pork. Separate the beef ribs. Place with the chicken pieces in a heavy-bottomed pot with the oil. Add onions, peeled and roughly chopped. Add the salt, peppercorns, bay leaf, and allspice.

Cover and simmer on low heat for at least 2–3 hours stirring occasionally until all the meat has become tender and the beef fallen off the ribs. Remove the bones and allow to cool.

Place the chicken livers and milk in another saucepan and bring to the boil. Drain and add to the meat.

Add the bread rolls, broken roughly into pieces, stirring so they soak up the meat juices. Grind the mixture into a smooth paste.

Preheat the oven to 180°C (350°F).

Stir the egg yolks into the meat mixture. Beat the egg whites until stiff, and then fold in. Add salt and pepper to taste.

Line 2 loaf tins 23 × 13 × 7 cm (9 × 5 × 3 in) with baking paper. Pour the mixture into the baking tins and bake for 20–30 minutes.

Leave the pasztet loaves in their tins to cool before turning them out. Serve cold slices of pasztet with ćwikła (horseradish relish, see page 168) or pickled cucumbers (see Rose Petal Jam, page 22).

*Ćwikła is a sharp-tasting relish made from horseradish and beetroot. The horseradish gives it heat and bite and the beetroot provides sweetness. This most popular of Polish relishes lends 'Christmas red' to any meats or paté on the table.*

ĆWIKŁA

# Beetroot (Beets) and Horseradish Relish

MAKES 1 SMALL JAR

1kg (about 2lb) beetroot (beets)
1 jar horseradish (approx 200 g)
1 teaspoon sugar
1 teaspoon salt
juice of ½ lemon

Peel, boil and grate the beetroot finely. Add horseradish to taste, for sharper flavour add more.

Stir in the sugar, salt and lemon juice and serve chilled.

Cheating allowed! Canned whole beetroot may be used and works well.

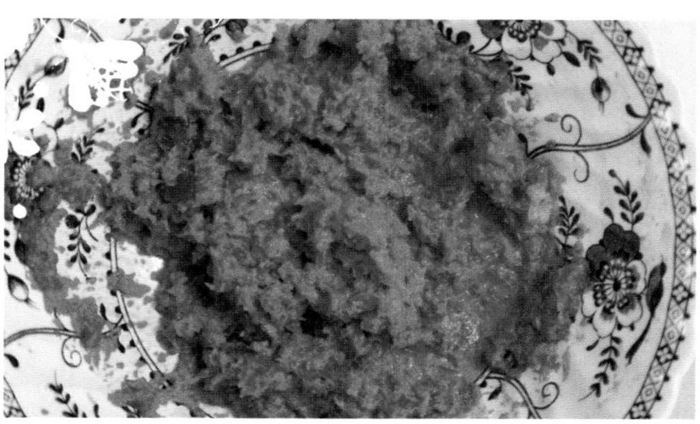

# The Land of Childhood

Today here for us, world's guests uninvited,
in all our future, and our past blighted,
there remains only one country, the sole
land where some gladness remains for a Pole!
Land of one's childhood! She only will prove
holy and pure, as the very first love;
never by memories of past errors hounded,
nor by illusion swayed of hopes unfounded,
nor by the stream of events soon confounded.

From *Pan Tadeusz: Epilogue*
by Adam Mickiewicz, 1834
(trans. Marcel Weyland)

# Kraj lat dziecinnych

***Dziś dla nas, w świecie nieproszonych gości,***
***W całej przeszłości i w całej przyszłości***
***Jedna już tylko jest kraina taka,***
***W której jest trochę szczęścia dla Polaka:***
***Kraj lat dziecinnych! On zawsze zostanie***
***Święty i czysty jak pierwsze kochanie,***
***Nie zaburzony błędów przypomnieniem,***
***Nie podkopany nadziei złudzeniem***
***Ani zmieniony wypadków strumieniem.***

ABOVE "Children with a *turoń* (Monster)" by Tadeusz Makowski, 1929.

A NEW YEAR

*With Christmas over all too soon I tried to keep the festive atmosphere at home for a little while longer. I looked after the Christmas tree, topped up the water in its stand, and swept away any fallen pine needles so no-one would dare to undress it.*

*With Christmas over all too soon I tried to keep the festive atmosphere at home for a little while longer. I looked after the Christmas tree, topped up the water in its stand, and swept away any fallen pine needles so no-one would dare to undress it.*

PN-62/D-94061

ZPZ CZECHOWICE PRZEC. 64 ZAP. 50 GR

I read my new books, given to me for Christmas, nestled next to Julia on the kitchen sofa. The Christmas lights danced on her white hands and turned her silver hair pink. She looked so pretty, not like the black widow I knew. Our cat, exhausted by all the Christmas fuss, slept on her lap, unaware that his shiny black fur had been turned into multi-coloured leopard skin by the Christmas tree's last sparkles.

The school holidays had finally begun and skiing and skating occupied all children's heads, with Olympic records waiting to be beaten.

# Ice Skates for Christmas

*When I was seven I received new ice skates for Christmas. The shiny, white leather boots had the permanent metal blades attached. Now I could give up my clumsy clip-ons and show off my new present. I was so proud of them I paraded around the town for several days, hanging them from my shoulder by long cotton shoelaces before finally dirtying them on the ice.*

Skating fever had started earlier in December. Every morning through the tightly shut window of my parents' kitchen I watched the silver line on the outside thermometer. I wanted it to drop as quickly as possible, into freezing temperatures, clearly marked in red for the heavens to see. But the slow and reluctant mercurial line would budge only a degree or so lower every few days. My school friends and I had to wait a little longer for that special event of the winter – the opening of our ice rink.

At the local stadium, the fire brigade pumped water over the soccer field to transform it into a rink for skating. Every day after school we inspected it through a wire fence hoping that the rock cast at it would not splash any water, but skid across like a Canadian ice hockey puck. Finally, one frozen wintry afternoon, the gates of the stadium opened, loudspeakers played "*O mnie się nie martw*"

("Don't worry about me") sung by Katarzyna Sobczyk and the fun began. Dizzy with excitement, we skated round and round the floodlit field ignoring soaking wet clothes, frozen fingers, and melting snowflakes in our hair, hoping to find our hats and gloves in tomorrow's daylight. The ice rink would melt and freeze, freeze and melt over the next few weeks, but we were never deterred by skating in slush.

Today many cities have ice rinks set out in their squares and shopping malls. Ice made in the 21st century shows clear contempt for outside temperatures and barometric highs. The kids still chase each other but in waterproof padded Gore-Tex. They are watched over by their parents and grandparents, hopefully nostalgic about their own skating, to 1960s music.

ABOVE "Waterfall" by G. Mattis, 1835.

*There is a long tradition in Poland of making teas from dried fruit and herbs. The tea from a rose hip looks pretty and pink and has a delicate taste and fragrance just right for a winter's tale shared between friends.*

## Herbata z dzikiej róży

# *Rose Hip Tea*

MAKES 2 LARGE CUPS OF TEA

- 2 tablespoons rose hips
- 2 cinammon sticks
- 1 teaspoon ground cloves
- 1 tablespoon honey or rose petal jam
- 2 tsps dried rose buds
- Slices of dried fruit – prune, fig, or apple (optional)

Put all the ingredients in a medium-sized saucepan and cover with fully boiling water.

Simmer on a very low heat for 2 minutes, then serve in large cups or thick glasses. Sweeten with honey or rose petal jam.

For extra flavour, various sliced dried fruit can be added, like apple, fig, prune or strawberry.

*My grandmother made ice cream in winter when the temperature dropped below minus 20. She used the kitchen windowsill as her freezer, on which she placed a large bowl of ice cream mixture. I watched the bowl impatiently, urged by my Mama Druga to stop opening the window and sticking my fingers into it. Thanks to the freezing Arctic fronts passing over our roof the ice cream set quickly and was scooped into my bowl without delay.*

## LODY POMARAŃCZOWE

# Orange Ice Cream

SERVES 8

- 8 pieces sugared orange peel (see page 32)
- 4 fresh oranges
- 600 ml (2½ cups) double or thickened cream
- 200 g (7 oz) icing (powdered) sugar
- 4 drops orange oil or essence
- pinch salt

Zest the oranges and squeeze out their juice. Mix zest and juice with sugar, stirring until dissolved. Add the orange oil or essence and a pinch of salt.

Dice the sugared orange peel into small 3mm (⅛ in) cubes.

Beat the cream until thick and forming firm peaks. Fold in the orange peel, and the juice and zest mix.

Pour into a sealable 2 litre (3 pint) plastic container and place in the freezer for 3 or 4 hours.

# *New Year's Eve – Sylwester*

*The week after Christmas was devoted to getting an outfit for the New Year's Eve ball, called Sylwester. In our city apartment block the old woman on the ground floor was a great pre-war tailor from Lwów. She could make a dress good enough for the Paris catwalks.*

I remember waiting for my 18-year-old aunt Elizabeth to have her first Sylwester ball gown fitted. Made of dark green lace lined with emerald-coloured silk, the creation was worthy of Scarlett O'Hara. I wished a handsome Rhett Butler would find her that night.

I was only an eight-year-old girl, and far too young for the ball, but I loved watching other women, young and old, crowding into the tailor's dining room. They sat patiently, hugging in their arms folded metres of precious fabrics: golden brocades, fine lace, and the softest of velvet. In my head I already wore their elegant dresses, and waltzed on the shiny parquet floors, "one, two, three – one, two, three".

Outside the tailor's apartment, the stairs were busy with women running up and down. They giggled and knocked on each other's doors, their fingers spread apart to dry their nail polish. Irons, hair dryers, rollers, and safety pins were borrowed and exchanged in preparation for the

ABOVE "Portrait of a Woman in a Black Dress" by Teodor Axentowicz, 1906.

most important ball of the year. On the second floor lived a young woman, Pani Basia, who wore large hoop earrings and played loud rock music. She could fix your hair into a "Brigitte Bardot do", requiring several cans of hairspray and the tiniest silver hairnet to keep it together until the ball.

Everyone knew that the old lonely widow on the top floor had a bottle of Chanel No.5 perfume. It had been sent to her from London by her brother, whom she hadn't seen since the Second World War. She awarded a dab to any woman brave enough to take her large boxer dog for a walk. Her dog Kora was a giant creature, with a mind of her own and the strength of an ox, who pulled poor women through slippery park alleys, past empty fountains, and across mountains of piled up snow. The risk of falling or losing the creature was well worth the few precious drops of ephemeral French fragrance on Polish décolletage.

It wasn't until I was 40 years old that I danced at my first Sylwester in Poland. I had returned home with my English husband and a Polish New Year's Eve ball was one of the attractions I had promised. The ball, in the village's old castle, started around 8pm with an elaborate five-course dinner, including a signature dish of roast turkey with juniper sauce. As soon as the dessert plates were removed the dancing started, with not a minute to be wasted on polite table conversation. Tirelessly enthusiastic dancers did not allow the band to take a break. I was relieved to find that the women dressed as elegantly as I remembered and the men were dashing and charmant, and always kissed their partners' hands when escorting them back to their tables.

RIGHT 1960s Polish dress patterns.

arnawa
5
6
7
8
Karnawał
Suknie
wieczorowe
balowe
ślubne
1962
55
10
WYDAWNICTWA SPECJALNE
„Świata Mody"

At midnight champagne corks popped and fireworks ripped the winter's night sky in zig zag patterns. Kissing and well-wishing lasted until 1am at which time my polite English husband started on his jolly goodbyes, causing surprised gazes among the assembled company. He was saved from ridicule by a burly waiter, who marched triumphantly into the ballroom carrying red barszcz and savoury croquettes. He urged Simon to sit down, eat, and recharge his batteries before setting out on a torch-lit sleigh ride (*kulig*).

Covered with blankets and sheepskin rugs we rode around the village cheering and singing, hoping that the frosty winter's air might help extinguish the champagne bubbles in our heads. Rosy cheeked and awake again we returned to the dance floor, dancing non-stop for another two hours, my husband now resigned to never going home. More food appeared on our table. Hunter's Stew (*Bigos*), vegetable salads, and steak tartare were piled up for us to snack on. 5am was time for breakfast, with scrambled eggs, wild mushrooms and freshly brewed coffee.

As we walked home that morning music still rang in our ears. Simon kept dancing and bragging that an Englishman can indeed dance, eat, and drink until dawn. His father, after all, he now recalled, was said to be the best waltzer in pre-war London. He was sure he could waltz even better than his father, undeterred by the icy Polish pathways... He proudly tried to get up again without asking for my helping hand.

We laughed and walked home slowly. We knew the sun would not wake up for at least another couple of hours. We looked up at the stars overhead, trying in vain to read their meaning and predict our future for the New Year ahead.

*This is a traditional way to cook turkey with a stuffing made of almonds, raisins and chałka bread. Serve with juniper sauce and roasted vegetables.*

INDYK PIECZONY

# Roast Turkey with Almond Stuffing

SERVES 8–10

1 turkey, c. 4.5 kg (10 lb)
3 tablespoons melted butter

FOR THE STUFFING

220 g (½ lb) stale chałka or any white bread
100 g (4 oz) chopped almonds
200 g (7 oz) sultanas (golden raisins)
100 ml (roughly 2 oz) dry breadcrumbs
2 tbs chopped parsley
1 teaspoon ground cloves
½ teaspoon nutmeg
0.5 l (about a pint) milk
2 eggs, beaten
50 g (2 oz) butter (softened)

Preheat the oven to 180°C (350°F).

Break the bread into small pieces. Combine with other stuffing ingredients in a large bowl and mix together well. Season with salt and pepper.

Fill turkey cavities with stuffing and close the openings with metal skewers. Place the turkey in a roasting tray. Brush with melted butter and sprinkle with salt.

Roast for 2 ½–3 hours, or about 20 minutes per 500 g (1 lb). Baste the turkey with juices from the pan every half hour. To prevent the meat from drying add a little hot water to the pan. If the skin is browning too quickly, cover loosely with foil.

Test when the turkey is cooked by inserting a thin skewer into the thickest part of the meat, the juices should run clear. Once cooked, remove the turkey from the oven and let it stand for 15 minutes.

Serve in slices with juniper sauce (see page 198) and spoonfuls of stuffing.

*In Polish cooking juniper berries are used to make a tangy sauce to accompany game dishes.*

SOS JAŁOWCOWY

# Juniper Sauce

SERVES 4

- 100 g (4 oz) bacon, finely chopped
- 1 onion, finely chopped
- 3 tablespoons juniper berries
- 1 carrot, finely diced
- 0.5 l (2 cups) chicken stock
- 250 ml (1 cup) dry white wine
- 25 g (1 oz) butter
- 1 tablespoon plain (all-purpose) flour
- 1 teaspoon lemon juice

Sauté the bacon, onion, juniper berries, and carrot together for 5 minutes on a medium heat.

Add the chicken stock and simmer on a low heat for 30 minutes.

Strain the liquid well.

Melt the butter in another saucepan on a low heat and slowly stir in the flour to make a roux. Add the juniper and vegetable liquid to the roux, followed by the wine, stirring continuously.

Turn up the heat and bring to the boil. As the sauce thickens add the lemon juice and salt and pepper to taste.

Serve hot, poured over slices of roast turkey (see page 196).

*These savoury pancakes are served after midnight at a New Year's Eve Ball. It is a true 'lunch' at 1 (a.m.) to keep you dancing till the shy dawn of the New Year's Day peers through ballroom windows.*

## BARSZCZ Z KROKIETEM

# Beetroot Soup with Savoury Croquette

Place beef with chopped carrots, one onion, celery, parsely and water in a large pot, bring to the boil and simmer for at least 90 minutes, until the meat is very soft. Remove beef, discard vegetables and keep liquid stock.

Grind meat and fry the onion in the oil. Put the meat and onion in a large saucepan, and stir in nutmeg, sour cream, butter, and dry breadcrumbs. Add 1 cup of the liquid stock. Heat gently for 10 minutes, stirring well to form a moist paste for the filling.

Make the pancakes by beating the eggs and milk together, then fold in the flour. Add a pinch of salt, cover, and set aside for 30 minutes.

Fry a dollop of the batter mix in butter to form a thin pancake. Cook for a minute on both sides.

Spread a thin layer of the meat filling over each pancake. Fold the pancake in on four sides to make a square, then roll up to make croquette shape.

Beat egg with a little water and paint each croquette before rolling in dry breadcrumbs. Fry the croquettes in a little butter for a minute on each side before serving with hot beetroot soup (barszcz, see page 148).

MAKES 8 CROQUETTES

1 kg gravy beef or chuck steak
3 carrots
2 tbs chopped parsely
2 onions
1 stick celery
2l (approx 4 pints) water
1 teaspoon nutmeg
1 tbs sour cream
1 tbs butter softened
1 tbs dry breadcrumbs
1 tbs vegetable oil

FOR THE PANCAKES

2 eggs
350 ml (12 fl oz) milk
300 g (11 oz) self-raising flour
50 g (2 oz) unsalted butter for frying
bread crumbs and beaten egg for coating

SPACER Z CZECHOWICZEM

UWAGA
DOBRY PIES
ALE MA
SŁABE NERWY

K+M+B

2013г.

PN-62/D-94061
LIS

WINTER HOLIDAYS

In early January, after Christmas together, my family parted. I joined my friends on a school camp, while my parents were granted precious time alone in the mountain resort in Karpacz. Józefa was busy in her caslte, delighting guests with sumptuous soups and dumplings.

*In early January, after Christmas together, my family parted. I joined my friends on a school camp, while my parents were granted precious time alone in the mountain resort in Karpacz. Józefa was busy in her castle, delighting guests with sumptuous soups and dumplings.*

Julia stayed home alone, safe behind a barricade of new books she got for Christmas. She promised to share them on our return from the snowy mountain slopes.

My husband planned our January expedition with a sailor's precision, on the biggest map of Poland we could find in Australia. While on the road we spent many wintry evenings staring at that map. It gathered mulled wine stains and became a hitchhiker's guide to a galaxy of dark pine forests, sleepy towns with abandoned castles, and vacant stork nests on telegraph poles.

PTTK
DZIANISZ
1h 30'
ZAKOPANE
1h
PTTK
Zakopane
PTTK
Zakopane
CHOCHOŁÓW
3h 15'

# *Karpacz*

*Sometimes my parents took me with them on 'wczasy' in the mountain village of Karpacz. 'Wczasy' were sponsored holidays that employees from a given workplace spent together in an allocated winter or summer resort.*

On the first night there was always a dance. It was called "an evening of introductions" (wieczorek zapoznawczy). Children were allowed to stay up and huddled together down one end of the hall to watch their parents spinning around to brassy music from a live band. My favourite song was "Jesteśmy na wczasach w tych góralskich lasach" ("We're on holidays in the mountain forests") by the singer Wojciech Młynarski. Its witty lyrics and sentimental music made everyone get up and dance, including the kitchen staff and waitresses. It was like an anthem that declared the winter holidays open.

Two weeks later the same band came back to provide music and romance for the farewell night (wieczorek pożegnalny). This was the symbolic end of the winter holidays for us, even if it was still only January and another group would be starting their holiday the very next day. On that final night the dancing went on long into the early hours while everyone said their sentimental goodbyes, forgetting they would be saying hello again on Monday morning back in their office or factory only 20 kilometres away.

LEFT 1970s Karpacz
LEFT INSET Scene from music video of 'Jesteśmy na wczasach'.

*From the top of the mountain in Karpacz one could clearly see a kiosk near the bottom of the ski lift, with a circle of skis planted like a picket fence around it. At lunchtime we slalomed there for a hot cup of soup. Tomato soup with rice was my favourite.*

## ZUPA POMIDOROWA Z RYŻEM

# Tomato Soup with Rice

Dice onion, carrot, celery, parsely, parsnip and swede. Gently saute in oil in a heavy bottomed pot. Blanch tomatoes in hot water for 5 minutes, rinse in cold water and peel off the skin.

Add tomatoes to the pot, pour in the stock. Boil for 20-30 minutes until the vegetables are soft. Add 2 tablespoons tomato paste, remove from heat and blend with a hand held blender. Stir in the cream and simmer for a couple more minutes. Do not boil.

Cook rice separately according to intructions on the packet. Drain rice but don't rinse with cold water, so it stays sticky. Fill a cup with rice and invert into soup bowl. Fill bowl with hot tomato soup.

SERVES 4

1 kg (2 lb 3 oz) tomatoes
1 medium-sized onion
2 tablespoons fresh flat leaf parsley
3 carrots
½ swede
1 parsnip
1 small stalk celery
3 tablespoons olive oil
2 tablespoons tomato paste
1 l (4 cups) chicken stock (bouillon)
400g (2 cups) long grain rice
200ml (½ pint) fresh cream

*There was a Hungarian restaurant in Jelenia Góra called "Tokaj". It was thought very fashionable and avant garde for being ethnic. Its specialty was a large potato pancake, covered with a thick meat goulash, folded over and served with a dash of sour cream. My parents drank 'Egri Bikaver' (Bull's Blood) red wine with their pancakes, while a local, virtuoso violinist played csardas.*

## PLACEK PO WĘGIERSKU

# *Hungarian Pancake with Goulash*

SERVES 6

FOR THE GOULASH
1 kg (c. 2 lb) pork neck
2 tbs plain (all-purpose) flour
3 onions, finely chopped
1 tablespoon hot paprika powder
120 ml (½ cup) cream
240 ml (1 cup) water
1 large carrot, diced
vegetable oil for frying

FOR POTATO PANCAKES
6 medium-sized potatoes
2 tablespoons plain (all-purpose) flour
1 egg, beaten
sour cream for serving plus marinated red peppers (if desired)

Cut the meat into 3 cm (1 in) cubes and place in a sealed plastic sandwich bag with the flour, shaking the bag gently to coat the meat evenly. Heat the oil in a heavy pan and brown the meat on all sides.

Remove the meat and fry the onion for a few minutes. Return the meat to the pan with the fried onion and add the paprika, the diced carrot, seasoning, and water and simmer for 30 minutes on a low heat or until the meat is tender. Stir in the cream.

To make the pancakes, peel and chop the potatoes, then purée them in the food processor. Mix in the flour and beaten egg, and season with salt and pepper.

Heat a little oil in a large frying pan (skillet). Pour batter in to make a thick (about 1 cm/½ in) pancake. Cook for 3 minutes on each side or until golden.

With the pancake still in the pan place a spoonful of goulash in a line across the middle then fold in half and cook for another minute.

Decorate if desired with slices of marinated red peppers. Serve hot with a dollop of sour cream.

# Książ

*Despite growing up in a communist country, where the working class was meant to be the ruling class, I couldn't help being fascinated by the life of an aristocrat, Daisy von Pless.*

This English princess lived in nearby Ksia̧ż Castle at the turn of the 20th century. Daisy had come to Lower Silesia from far away England to marry a handsome German prince. I couldn't resist the tales of her lavish parties and priceless jewels. When walking on school trips through her ballroom and gardens aged ten, I wanted to be a princess too. I was secretly ready to trade my scout uniform and red scarf for a chiffon dress with ostrich feathers.

Only now, after reading her biography, do I realize how much Daisy missed her home country and how difficult her marriage had been. Most importantly, I learned about her brave efforts to stop the First World War, through her friendships with both Emperor Wilhelm II and Edward VII of England. Her death, during World War 2, and the location of her grave remain a mystery.

The castle still rules proudly over the low-lying villages of a now democratic Poland, from the top of a mountain wrapped in garden terraces like a ballerina's tutu. When I walk there with my husband I imagine Princess Daisy again, in her long fur coat, taking her children for a walk in the snow.

LEFT Princess Daisy with her sons, Hansel & Aleksander, c.1906. ABOVE Książ Castle.

*This is my favourite piernik recipe, for a particularly soft and moist gingerbread, as made by my cousin's wife Małgosia. Like many young Polish cooks, Małgosia gets her best recipes from the internet, this one comes originally from the beautiful Polish cooking site 'White Plate.'*

## PIERNIK

# *Gingerbread Cake*

SERVES 8–10

120 g (4½ oz) dark cooking chocolate
120 g (4½ oz) butter
120 g (4½ oz) honey
80 g (3 oz) caster (superfine) sugar
120 ml (½ cup) milk
2 eggs
200 g (7 oz) plain (all-purpose) flour
100 g (4 oz) soft prunes, finely chopped
2 tsp gingerbread spice
1 tsp ground ginger
1 tsp cinnamon
2 tsp baking powder
40 g (1½ oz) candied ginger, chopped
½ jar (c. 120 g (4 ½ oz)) plum butter (powidła) or strawberry jam
2 tbs dry breadcrumbs

Melt the chocolate then place in a saucepan with the butter, honey, and sugar on a medium heat. Add the milk and stir together well until the sugar has dissolved. Set aside to cool.

Beat the eggs and fold them into the chocolate mixture.

In a large bowl combine the flour, chopped prunes, gingerbread spice, ground ginger, cinnamon, and baking powder. Mix well and stir in the chocolate and egg mixture, the plum butter or jam, and the crystallized (candied) ginger.

Preheat the oven to 160°C (310°F). Grease and flour a 28 cm (11 in) loaf tin. Dust with the breadcrumbs. Pour in the batter and bake for 60 minutes until slightly firm on the outside but still soft and moist inside. Allow to cool in the baking tin.

Wrap in plastic film and leave for a day before eating, in thick slices.
The gingerbread will keep well so you can make it a few days before Christmas.

*Pork Pot Roast is a slow cooked meal served with mashed potato and sweet boiled carrots. It makes a warming winter lunch when the family gathers together, despite the frost and snow that try to keep them apart.*

## PIECZEŃ WIEPRZOWA Z MARCHEWKĄ NA SŁODKO

# *Pork Pot Roast with Sweet Carrots*

SERVES 8

1 pork neck, 1–1.5kg (c. 2–3 lb)
1 tablespoon sweet paprika
2 large onions
2 bay leaves
4 cloves garlic, crushed
6 whole allspice berries
4 large carrots
0.5–0.75 l (2–3 cups) water
olive oil for frying

Rub the pork neck with the paprika, season with salt and pepper, leave in the fridge for 2 hours. Heat a little olive oil in a heavy-bottomed pot and brown the pork neck on all sides.

Add chopped onions, bay leaves, crushed garlic, allspice, and water.

Put the lid on the pot and let it simmer for 2 hours on a low heat or until the meat is very soft and tender. Add more water during cooking if the meat starts to dry out.

Peel & boil carrots until tender, then dice and saute in melted butter with a teaspoon of caster (superfine) sugar. Serve pork with carrots, and mashed potatoes.

PKP cargo
GRUPA PKP
Pt-47

P.K.P
Pług odśnież

# Wolsztyn

Forget the romance and mystery of Książ Castle, Wolsztyn is where my husband really wants to go - one of the last places in Europe that still operates a scheduled steam locomotive service. Crawling under giant steam engines that reek of coal tar and hot steam, that's what life is really all about. Strangely there are no women here, only 40+-year-old boys, playing with hissing pistons and grease guns. If they are good they are allowed to drive one of these thundering machines, far away from their day jobs, health and safety regulations, and wives.

# The Locomotive

**A big locomotive has pulled into town,**
**Heavy, humungus, with sweat rolling down,**
**A plump jumbo olive.**
**Huffing and puffing and panting and smelly,**
**Fire belches forth from her fat cast iron belly.**
**Poof, how she's burning,**
**Oof, how she's boiling,**
**Puff, how she's churning,**
**Huff, how she's toiling.**
**She's fully exhausted and all out of breath,**
**Yet the coalman continues to stoke her to death.**

# Lokomotywa

***Stoi na stacji lokomotywa,***
***Ciężka ogromna i pot z niej spływa -***
***Tłusta oliwa.***
***Stoi i sapie, dyszy i dmucha,***
***Żar z rozgrzanego jej brzucha bucha:***
***Buch - jak gorąco!***
***Uch - jak gorąco!***
***Puff - jak gorąco!***
***Uff - jak gorąco!***
***Już ledwo sapie, już ledwo zipie,***
***A jeszcze palacz węgiel w nią sypie.***

**Julian Tuwim, 1938, extract**
**trans. Walter Whipple**

*Beef rissoles with potatoes were on the menu in every kindergarten and school canteen when I was a child. I loved mashing the rissoles and potato together into a delicious mess. Different rules applied at home, where rissoles were beautifully presented with mashed potato and salad on the side, to be eaten politely with a knife and fork.*

## KOTLETY MIELONE

## *Beef Rissoles*

SERVES 6

- 1 kg (c. 2 lb) minced beef
- 1 onion, chopped finely
- 1 egg
- 2 cloves garlic, crushed
- 2 small stale bread rolls soaked in water
- ½ teaspoon chilli powder or dried chilli flakes (optional)
- 120 ml (½ cup) water
- olive oil for frying

Mix together all the ingredients in a large bowl.

Using a spoon and your hands, shape the mince into small, slightly flattened balls the size of golf balls.

Heat the oil on a medium heat and fry the rissoles for a few minutes in batches to brown them all round.

Fill a large saucepan with the browned rissoles, then add the water. Cover and simmer on a low heat for 10 minutes to cook through.

Serve hot with mashed potato or as a hearty cold lunch with bread.

# Baltic Sea

*The little towns along the coast are quiet and dreamy in January. All loud music and the smell of fried flathead has been stored away until next summer, together with stacks of creaking wicker chairs, and neon-coloured plastic lilos.*

Sometimes the Baltic Sea is sleepy and content, under a cosy blanket of ice, but when the Arctic wind provokes, it wakes again, angry and frustrated, cracking its icy shackles. Our long walks on the beach in winter are rewarded by Neptune himself. He offers up handfuls of caramel-coloured amber, and sprinkles them along the lacy edges of the waves. Such precious jewels would never be granted on our Australian Pacific shores.

*These delicate pastry shells filled with smooth custard are well worth the effort. Muszelki always disappear instantly from the table, as if washed away by a big wave of the Baltic Sea.*

## MUSZELKI

# Sea Shells

MAKES ABOUT 16

FOR THE PASTRY

5 egg yolks
1 tsp caster (superfine) sugar
1 tsp (½ oz) unsalted butter
2 tsps thick sour cream
2 tsps white vinegar
500 g (1 lb 4 oz) plain (all-purpose) flour
vegetable oil for deep frying
icing (powdered) sugar for decoration

FOR THE CRÈME FILLING

3 whole eggs
225 g (8 oz) caster (superfine) sugar
0.5 l (2 cups) milk
2 tablespoons potato flour
5 tablespoons (2 ½ oz) vanilla sugar

To make the pastry, cream together the egg yolks, sugar, butter, sour cream, and vinegar. Sift in the flour little by little to form an elastic dough.

Roll out the dough to a thickness of 3 mm (⅛ in). Use an inverted tumbler to cut out 6 cm (2 ½ in) circles. Repeat until all the dough is used.

Deep fry the pastry circles in hot oil until golden on both sides. Remove and drain on paper towels.

To make the crème filling, beat the eggs with the sugar until fluffy. Fold in the flour.

Gently heat the milk with the vanilla sugar until the sugar has dissolved. Remove from the heat and allow to cool slightly. Gradually stir into the egg and sugar mixture.

Take half of the cooked pastry circles and place a teaspoon of crème filling on each. Place the remaining circles on top to form lids like seashells, lightly pressing around the edges.

Just before serving, sprinkle with icing sugar for decoration.

# *Mazury Lakes in Winter*

*The Mazury Lakes in January are only for those in search of peace and solitude. We drive alone on narrow winding roads that cruelly part brotherly lakes, separated at their glacial birth millions of winters ago.*

Frozen, silver grey waters stretch into the distance, grasping the snowy skies, sealing the world into a crystal ball, with only us, like prehistoric insects, trapped inside. We try to crack the surface of the icy lakes with pebbles and sticks. They slide for a few seconds but stall, dutifully obeying Newtonian rules. The stillness and composure of the lake are immediately restored and we are overwhelmed by the silence around us. We whisper to each other, our words kissing on dragon's breath between our lips.

ABOVE The Ranger's Cottage (Leśniczówka 'Pranie') home of Polish poet Konstantyn Ildefons Gałczyński.

Small villages and towns feel deserted. Only faint white wood smoke, rising above red-tiled roofs, gives away the presence of locals hiding from snow and lost tourists. A restaurant seems to be open, despite its door being barricaded by stacks of kayaks and pedallos. A sleepy chef, like a hibernating bear disturbed before spring, looks up with surprise at our arrival "in the wrong season". He rewards our winter visit to Mazury with warming smoked salmon and cheese soup, kartacze (meat and potato dumplings) and apple mousse, a truly hearty meal for arctic explorers from the tropical antipodes. We promise to return when the lakes thaw and the kayaks are afloat again.

*This fish soup, popular in winter can be made with smoked or red, canned salmon. Cheese and cream make it rich – which is allowed after a day spent skating or skiing.*

ZUPA SEROWA Z ŁOSOSIEM

# *Salmon and Cheese Soup*

ENOUGH FOR 4

1 × 450 g (1 lb) can red salmon (or fresh smoked salmon)
1 l (c. 2 pints) chicken stock
1 stick (rib) celery
1 leek
2 cloves garlic, crushed
25 g (1 oz) butter
1 teaspoon rosemary
3 teaspoons sour cream
120 ml (½ cup) thickened or heavy cream
100 g (4 oz) grated cheddar cheese
2 teaspoons fresh dill
freshly ground black pepper

Melt the butter in a heavy-bottomed saucepan. Finely chop celery, garlic and leak and sauté over a medium heat for 6–8 minutes until they soften.

Stir in the chicken stock, salmon, and finely chopped rosemary and bring to the boil.

Remove from the heat and stir in the cheese, all the cream, the chopped dill and black pepper. Simmer gently for 5 minutes.

Serve hot with bread.

POKOJE

*This old Mazurian recipe is made with both cooked and raw potato. These giant, meat-filled gnocchi get their name from their shape, a bit like artillery shell cartridges. They are a traditional folk food in Poland's lake district.*

KARTACZE

# Meat and Potato "Shell Cartridges"

SERVES 4

- 250g (9 oz) beef mince
- 250g (9 oz) pork mince
- 1 onion
- 1 tablespoon chopped parsley
- 1 tablespoon chopped dill
- 1.5 kg (3 ¼ lb) dry, starchy potatoes
- 4 cloves garlic, crushed
- up to 200g (7oz) potato flour
- 100g (c. 4oz) fried chopped bacon or pancetta for serving
- olive oil for frying onion

Peel the potatoes. Boil half until tender, drain well. Put these cooked potatoes through a moulis or food processor to make a fine mash. Grate the remaining (raw) potatoes very finely by hand or in a food processor. Squeeze through a muslin cloth (cheesecloth) to remove all the moisture. Add to the cooked mash and season with salt. Mix well with your hands, and add potato flour until you have a firm, dry dough, like modelling clay.

Peel and chop the onion finely. Fry in a little oil for a couple of minutes until soft. Mix with the beef and pork mince in a bowl. Add in the garlic, parsley and dill. Season with salt and pepper.

Take a lump of the potato dough in your hand, enough to make a disc about 10cm (4 in) in diameter and 1 cm (½ in) thick. Place a teaspoon of the meat mix in the middle and fold the potato over to enclose it, pinching the edges together to seal. Now form into a ball and roll into the elongated 'cartridge' shape, with pointed ends. Repeat with the rest of the potato and meat.

Carefully place each kartacze in a large pot of boiling salted water. Boil for 15 minutes, remove and drain well. Kartacze are delicious served with fried chopped pancetta or bacon, and a carrot and cabbage salad.

*Neat rows of apples stored for winter spilled out of the cellar onto our pantry shelves, the kitchen window sill, old wooden dresser and living room bookcases. Spaced carefully apart, they fenced off volumes of Tolstoy and Sienkiewicz that I had promised Julia I would read. They transformed our house into an indoor orchard, while the apple trees outside dreamed of spring.*

## MUS Z JABŁEK

# *Apple Mousse*

SERVES 6–8

1 kg (2 lb 3 oz) cooking (baking) apples
100 g (4 oz) caster (superfine) sugar
1 lemon
240 ml (1 cup) water
5 egg whites
1 × 10 g (½ oz) packet gelatin
120 ml (½ cup) whipping cream
3–4 tablespoons sugared orange peel, very finely chopped (see page 32)
slices of apple to decorate

Peel and core the apples.

Place the apples in a large pan with the sugar, ½ cup water, the zest and juice of the lemon. Simmer for 10 minutes, covered, or until the apple is soft.

Beat the egg whites until stiff. Dissolve the gelatin in the remaining ½ cup water.

Use an electric beater to purée the apple, adding the cream and the dissolved gelatin as you beat.

Carefully fold in the chopped orange peel and the beaten egg whites.

Pour into a round jelly mould and refrigerate for 4 hours.

Turn out of the mould when set and decorate with slices of apple. Serve with whipped cream, if desired.

# *Białystok*

*Catholic and Orthodox Christians live side by side in the peaceful eastern town of Białystok. Christmas here can be celebrated twice, with the festive season stretching well into the New Year.*

Onion-domed churches and Catholic bell towers and spires share the winter skies with soaring birds. God doesn't seem to mind if you cross yourself to the right or left, write his name in a Latin or Cyrillic alphabet. He doesn't seem to be concerned whether Christmas falls in December or January, as long as people love each other as per his commandment, written first in Hebrew.

OPPOSITE Orthodox Church of the Holy Spirit, Białystok.

LEFT Old Russian postcard 'East or West - home is the best'.

*This popular herring salad has travelled across the eastern border. In Russian* Селедка под шубой *means 'salad under a fur coat', as a layer of mayonnaise gives the appearance of a white fur coat.*

## SZUBA

# *Russian salad 'under a fur coat'*

MAKES 4

- 2 salted herring fillets
- 3 fresh beetroot (beets)
- 3 carrots
- 4 potatoes
- 1 red onion
- 4 eggs
- 200ml (about 7 fl oz) mayonnaise
- parsley and dill to decorate

Boil or bake the beetroot until cooked. Allow to cool then peel. Peel potatoes and carrots, then boil until they are tender but firm enough to cut. Hard boil the eggs. Rinse the herring fillets, pat dry with paper towel then cut into small pieces.

Chop the eggs, potatoes, onion, beetroot and 2 of the carrots finely. Use a ring or cake mould (about 12cm or 5 inches) to help build your salad. First layer the potato and onion on the bottom, pressing own firmly, then 2 tablespoons of mayonnaise. Next build a layer of the herring pieces, a little more mayonnaise then the chopped egg. Then add the carrot, a drop more mayonnaise and the beetroot. Decorate the top with a thick coat of mayonnaise. Refrigerate overnight.

When ready to serve, remove the mold carefully and garnish with parsley and dill, and the remaining carrot, sliced.

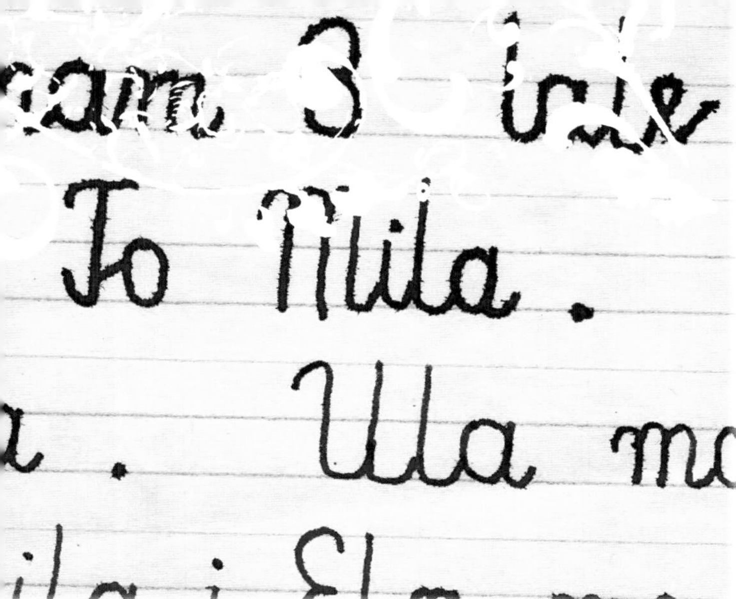
To Mila.
Ula

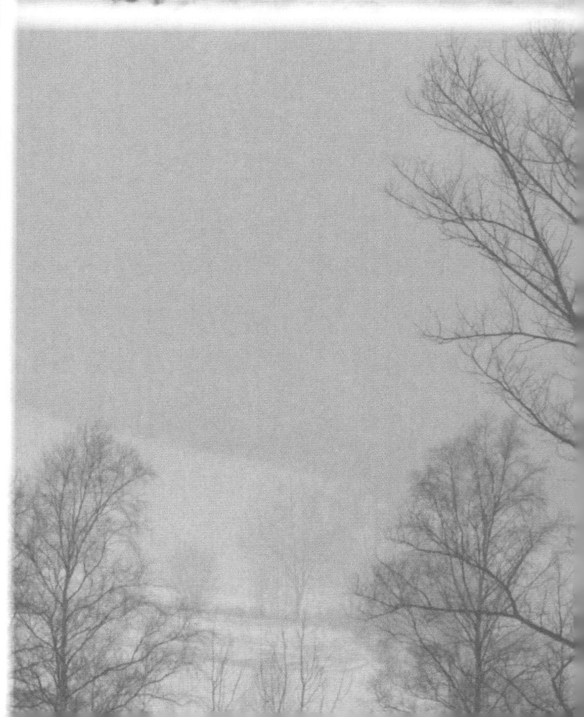

# *Tykocin*

*In Tykocin we admire the intricate Baroque ceilings of the Holy Trinity Church and the Hebrew prayers inscribed on the walls of the Baroque Jewish synagogue.*

Two such magnificent buldings in one small Polish town make me think about how Poles and Jews have lived side by side in Poland for centuries. Our food, music, poetry, language and DNA have been intertwined for 1000 years. Millions perished during the last world war and only a few returned to those two baroque temples to pray.

Back in 1943, before that war had ended, Polish poet Władysław Broniewski wrote this poem, promising a free Poland, a country of noble-minded citizens.

**Upon us and ruins of Warsaw one sun only shall shine,**
**When with a bloody victory our toil at last shall be ended:**
**To grant freedom, and bread and justice to all humankind,**
**And then one race on shall rise: the highest: men noble-minded.**

***Wspólne zaświeci nam niebo nad zburzoną Warszawą,***
***gdy zakończymy zwycięstwem krwawy nasz trud wieloletni:***
***każdy człowiek otrzyma wolność, kęs chleba i prawo***
***i jedna powstanie rasa, najwyższa: ludzie szlachetni.***

from 'To the Polish Jews'
by Władysław Broniewski, 1943 (trans. Marcel Weyland)

OPPOSITE Holy Trinity Church, Tykocin

*This is my Aunt Elizabeth's recipe for apple cake. Sweet, succulent spicy apples are enclosed in a thin layer of soft pastry. It is rarely served cold, as it does not get much chance to cool down.*

## SZARLOTKA

# *Apple Charlotte*

SERVES 6–8

180 g (6 oz) unsalted butter
100 g (4 oz) icing (powdered) sugar
225 g (8 oz) plain (all-purpose) flour
1 egg yolk
3 tablespoons thick or heavy cream
1.5 kg (c. 3 lb) apples
1 teaspoon lemon juice
225 g (8 oz) caster (superfine) sugar
1 tsp cinnamon
1 tsp ground cloves

For the pastry: Cut the butter into small cubes and blend with the sugar and flour in a large bowl. Mix the egg yolk with 1 tablespoon of the cream and stir in. Knead the dough with your hands to blend all the ingredients well. Shape into a ball, wrap in plastic film, and refrigerate for 1 hour.

For the filling: Peel and cube the cooking apples and place in a heavy-bottomed saucepan. Cover partially and cook with the lemon juice over a low heat until the apple is starting to soften and most of the juices have evaporated. Stir in the sugar, cloves and cinnamon and allow to cool.

On a floured board, roll out two thirds of the dough, no more than 5 mm (¼ in) thick, to form a 35 cm (14 in) circle. Use this to line a 30cm (12 in) cake tin, running the surplus up the sides. Refrigerate for 40 minutes. Preheat the oven to 190°C (375 °F).

Blind bake for 20 minutes (covering the pastry with baking paper and filling with dried beans or rice). Allow to cool.

Pour in the apple filling. Make thin strips of pastry from the remaining dough and place across the top to form a lattice. Prick with a fork and brush the remaining cream over the pastry and bake for a further 30 minutes or until the filling is bubbling. Serve warm with custard or whipped cream.

# Białowieża

*On a grey, January morning we visit Białowieża in search of the famous European bison that still inhabit Europe's oldest forest, the Puszcza Białowieska.*

Our hotel has written instructions in the guest information folder on how to behave if confronted by a bison. As neither of us are bison whisperers, we opt for the safer option of meeting them in the nearby reserve.

We drive for some distance off the main road and into the forest. The excited cashier is surprised to see visitors on such a cold day. While walking through the empty alleys of the reserve we get a fair idea about the structure of this corporation, in which the cashier appears to be the only human. The Executive Director is clearly the bison, an unapproachable, old, and stately figure, unmoved by our waves and smiles. The Public Relations Representative is the elk, who shadows us along the fence, voicing his appreciation for our unexpected visit. The accounts are kept in secret by a sly, unblinking lynx, while Ground Maintenance is left to Tarpan horses and wild boars. All this happens under Surveillance and Security provided by a family of wolves. I would like to be here on Christmas Eve, the one day of the year that these animals can speak, and hear their stories about the two Australian tourists who rolled in the frozen mud trying to photograph them.

*My great grandmother Julia dried wild mushrooms for winter in the attic. Long garlands of shrivelling mushrooms hung down from high wooden beams and their foresty scent descended quietly on our sleepy household at night. My Christmas gołąbki recipe uses fresh mushrooms, and is served with a thick mushroom sauce for extra mushroom flavour.*

## GOŁĄBKI Z GRZYBAMI

# Cabbage Rolls with Mushrooms and Rice

MAKES 10 ROLLS

FOR THE FILLING

450g (1lb) fresh mushrooms finely diced
250 g (8 oz) long grain rice
1 onion, chopped finely
1 whole Savoy cabbage
1 egg, beaten
25 g (1 oz) butter
1 tablespoon olive oil
200 ml (7 fl oz) water

FOR THE MUSHROOM SAUCE

225g (8 oz) mushrooms finely chopped
30g (1 oz) butter
350 ml (½ pint) vegetable stock
1 tablespoon flour
1 tablespoon cream

Fry the mushrooms and onion in the butter until the onion is soft and golden brown. Cook the rice according to instructions on the packet, drain but do not rinse, so it stays sticky. Let it cool for a moment then combine the rice with the fried mushrooms and onion, and the beaten egg. Season with salt and pepper and mix well together.

Soften the cabbage leaves by boiling the whole cabbage in a large saucepan of salted water for 10 minutes. Drain and allow to cool before peeling off individual leaves. Use a knife to cut out any thick white veins in the cabbage leaves to make them easier to fold.

Place about a tablespoon of the mushroom and rice mixture on each cabbage leaf, then fold the leaf in a couple of times and roll to make a little parcel. Keep some cabbage leaves as you will need these later to line the saucepan.

Pour the olive oil in a large saucepan and add about 1 cm (½ in) of water. Line the pan with some cabbage leaves, then add the wrapped parcels. Cover with another layer of cabbage leaves. Pour in 200 ml (7 fl oz) of cold water then cover and bring to the boil. As soon as the water boils, lower the heat and simmer gently for about 45 minutes to steam the cabbage rolls.

To make the mushroom sauce, fry the extra mushrooms in the butter for 5 minutes. Add the flour and cook for another minute stirring well. Add the stock, bring to the boil and simmer for ten minutes until the sauce has thickened. Stir in the cream.

To serve, place 1 or 2 *gołąbki* (cabbage rolls) on each plate, then pour over the steaming mushroom sauce at the table.

POCZTA

OCZT

# *Tarnów*

*The beautiful and unspoiled medieval town of Tarnów waits to be discovered by tourists. Sometimes they get lost here on the way to Kraków and are caught in a labyrinth of cobblestoned streets.*

One of these streets has life sized statues of Polish poets - Osiecka, Herbert, and Brzechwa. Three humble figures sit on the bench among the passing crowds. The tourists may sit next to them while checking their map, but remember some poems instead, perhaps a better guide for a lost traveler.

Tarnów has a unique museum dedicated to Romani culture. Gypsy caravans (tabors), craft, colourful costumes and paintings are all on display. I hum 'Jadą wozy kolorowe taborami' (The colourful tabors are on the move again) a 1970s song sung by my favourite Polish female singer Maryla Rodowicz. This seductive and nostalgic song made me yearn for romance, adventure and travel, at a time when the Iron Curtain was still firmly shut over our mountain horizon.

ABOVE 'Cyganka' (Gypsy Woman) I.Tarczałowicz 1889

*This is a slow-cooked meat dish, so you have plenty of time to dream about travelling on a gypsy tabor while waiting for it to be ready. The flaky, tender meat is coated with a slightly sour and creamy gravy.*

PIECZEŃ WOŁOWA

# Sour braised beef

Serves 8

- 2 medium-sized onions
- 1 bay leaf
- 25 whole peppercorns
- 12 whole all spice (ziele angielskie)
- 750 ml (1½ cups) white vinegar
- 1.5 l (6 cups) water
- 1 kg (c. 2 lbs) "Scotch" beef fillet or silverside
- 300 ml (1 ¼ cups) single or pouring cream
- 1 tablespoon plain (all-purpose) flour
- olive oil for frying

Simmer sliced onion, bay leaf, peppercorns, all spice, vinegar, and all the water for 15 minutes, let it cool. Place the beef fillet in the marinade, spooning some over the top, and refrigerate overnight.

Preheat the oven to 180°C (350°F). Remove the meat from the marinade and pat dry with a paper towel. Rub with salt and pepper then brown on all sides in an oven proof saucepan in sizzling olive oil.

Once browned, add enough marinade to come halfway up the meat. Reserve remaining marinade for sauce. Bake in the oven for 3 hours, turning once, until the liquid has nearly evaporated and the meat is very tender.

Remove the meat and rest it for 30 minutes. Strain juices and return to saucepan. Make a smooth paste with the flour and half a cup of marinade. Add to the juices and beat with the cream over low heat to make a thick sauce, add more marinade as desired. Season with salt and pepper. Return sliced meat to the sauce, ready to serve with pasta and vegetables. Traditionally served with kopytka (see page 276) and pureed beetroot.

*Polish gnocchi are shaped a bit like horses hooves, and known as kopytka. Cut diagonally from a long roll of dough; the length is not prescriptive. They are delicious whatever their size.*

KOPYTKA

# *Polish Gnocchi "Little Hooves"*

SERVES 4 AS A SIDE DISH

5 medium-sized, starchy potatoes
1 egg
150–225 g (5–8 oz) potato flour
1 teaspoon salt
plain (all-purpose) flour for flouring board

Peel and boil the potatoes in salted water, mash, and allow to cool. Place them on a floured wooden board then add 150 g (5 oz) potato flour on top.

Make a well in the centre of the mixture and add the egg. Now add the salt and mix it all together with your hands. Add more potato flour as needed to make a light, springy potato dough.

Take a lump of dough and roll it out into a tube, about 3 cm (1 in) in diameter. Cut this diagonally into 5 cm (roughly 2 in) lengths.

Boil a large saucepan of salted water and add the kopytka. They are cooked when they float to the surface, after about 2 minutes.

Serve as a main meal with fried onion and butter (school cafeteria style) or as a side dish for Sour braised beef (see page 273). These Polish gnocchi go well with any sauce.

20

# Łódź

*Walking down the 5km long Piotrkowska Street feels like strolling though a movie set, which could be true, given Łódź is famous for its film school and studios.*

But the set is real. The grand old buildings with ornamental balconies and turrets are lessons in the architecture of the past two centuries, when the city's economy was booming.

Artur Rubinstein, Poland's favourite pianist and "Chopinist" was born in Łódź. Rubinstein family memorabilia, including posters and letters were donated by the pianist's wife Aniela (Nela) and are displayed in Izrael Poznański's palace, on Ogrodowa Street. Here we find The Nela Rubinstein Cookbook. It contains many Polish dishes, including desserts such as Lemon Bavarian Cream and Chocolate Mousse, that she used to make for her husband and their glamorous guests. Perhaps her mazurek, the traditional Polish cake - was the secret to his passionate and inspired performances of Chopin.

OPPOSITE Piotrkowska Street, Łódź in January. RIGHT Artur Rubinstein.

PAŃSTWOWA FILHARMONIA w ŁODZI
ODZNACZONA HONOROWĄ ODZNAKĄ m. ŁODZI
DYREKTOR I KIEROWNIK ARTYSTYCZNY – STEFAN MARCZYK
SEZON KONCERTOWY 1966/67
ŚRODA, DNIA 14-go WRZEŚNIA 1966 ROKU, GODZINA 19,30
RECITAL FORTEPIANOWY
ARTUR
RUBINSTEI
W PROGRAMIE L. VAN BEETHOVEN, F. CHOPIN, CL. DEBUSSY, M.
AL. E. CHABRIER, E. GRANDOS, F. LISZT.
Bilety w cenie zł 30–90 nabywać można w kasie Filharmonii w godz. 15–19;

Pola
NEGRI
A Woman Commands
ROLAND YOUNG

*Reading while eating chocolate would have to be my favourite winter activity, when the weather outside forces you to such hardship. This is a recipe to entertain kids, but for big kids some liqueur can be added instead of the orange juice.*

MUS CZEKOLADOWY

# *Chocolate Mousse*

SERVES 12

250 g (9 oz) good quality dark cooking chocolate
120 ml (½ cup) orange juice (or Kahlua or orange liqueur of your choice)
2 tablespoons caster (superfine) sugar
120 ml (½ cup) thick or heavy cream
zest of 2 oranges
5 eggs, separated

Melt the chocolate in the microwave (or in a small bowl over very hot water) then stir in the orange juice (or liqueur) and the sugar.

Transfer to a saucepan on a very low heat and add the cream and orange zest.

Remove from the heat, allow to cool a little, then stir in the egg yolks.

Beat the egg whites until stiff, and gently fold into the chocolate mixture trying to keep it light and airy.

Pour the mousse into individual bowls or ramekins. Chill in the fridge for at least 2 hours.

Decorate with sugared orange peel (see page 32) if desired.

OPPOSITE Children's poems by Jan Brzechwa, 1938

BRZECHWA
DZIECIOM

*A mazurek is a Polish dance, which Chopin often used in his piano works. It has three beats to a bar with a back beat on the third, a sort of classical prototype of rock and roll. It is also a much-loved Polish shortbeard tart made for both Christmas and Easter.*

## MAZUREK

# Orange Shortbread Tart

SERVES 6–8

- 100 g (4 oz) potato flour
- 200 g (8 oz) plain (all purpose) flour
- 90 g (4 oz) icing (powdered) sugar
- 2 egg yolks
- 150 g (5 oz) cold chopped butter
- 1 tablespoon thickened cream
- 150 g (5 oz) apricot jam
- 150 g (5 oz) orange marmalade
- 5 tbs chopped orange peel (see page 32)
- 4 tablespoons icing (powdered) sugar for decoration

Blend chopped butter, egg yolks, potato flour, plain flour and sugar in a food processor or by rubbing together with your fingers. Mix in the cream.

Roll the pastry (pie shell) into a ball, wrap in plastic food wrap, and refridgerate for an hour.

Preheat the oven to 180°C (350°F). Roll out the pastry into a rectangle 22 × 30 cm (9 × 12 in), about 5 mm (¼in) thick. Use the remaining pastry to cut out stars or whatever decorative shapes you like and position these around the edges of the rectangle, pressing them lightly into position. Slide the rectangle onto baking paper on a baking tray and prick over the pastry with a fork. Bake for 20 minutes until a light golden brown.

Remove the pastry and allow to cool. Mix the apricot jam and orange marmade with the chopped orange peel. Spread the jam mix evenly over the top.

Mix a little water with the icing sugar to make a runny icing to decorate the top, along with any spare sugared orange if desired.

Kwiaty
Praski Ogródek
MIECZYSŁAW
FOGG
ZNANE PRZEBOJE
oryginalne
nagrania z płyt
z lat trzydziestych
XX wieku

# Praga

*It is the last night of our winter holiday in Poland, tomorrow I must leave the country I grew up in and return to our present home in Australia. But first, our friend in Warsaw, Pola, takes us on a pub crawl through the bars of Praga.*

Across the Vistula river from Warsaw's Old Town, the Stalinist architecture here may appear cold and austere but the atmosphere in Praga's bars and restaurants is far from chilly. Maudlin migrants are always welcome. Cosy and inviting, these hideaways are often unmarked and located in unusual places, such as old factories, grocery stores, and apartment buildings, so it pays to have a local guide like Pola. Inside the first bar we are welcomed with a shot of clear Polish vodka (called Czysta ojczysta on the bar menu).

The music playing is the tango 'That Last Sunday' ('Ta ostatnia niedziela') a 1930's hit sung by Mieczysław Fogg. There is no Warsaw without Fogg's music as there is no Paris without Edith Piaf. I know his songs so well. Mama Druga played his records all the time. Fogg's sentimental tunes and tender lyrics took her back to pre-war Poland, when her husband Rudolph held her in his arms on the dance floor, long before his army uniform was sewn.

OPPOSITE Musical figures outside a Praga flower shop: passers by can send a text to hear them play the tango.

We drink and I reminisce about 'zielona noc' (The Green Night) the last night on school camps and holidays, when mischievous adventures took place, while our teachers slept. I remember how we snuck out of tents and gathered under the stars to dance in our pajamas, our faces smudged with toothpaste, fluorescent in the torchlight. When lights came on in the teachers' tent we quickly scrambled back to our beds, our blankets muffling our giggles. Next morning we slept on the bus home, waking only when the driver honked his horn at our parents, who waited patiently outside the school gates. After three weeks of separation they were ready to fold us in their arms and take us home to listen to our tall tales.

It's early morning when we get back to our hotel in the Old Town, only to pick up our suitcases and head for Okęcie, Warsaw's international airport. I watch the sleeping city from a frosted taxi window. I feel tired, though I know I shall sleep on the plane just as I used to doze on the bus after our final "green night".

OPPOSITE 'Primavera' mural in Praga.

*The bars of Praga will serve you any cocktail you can think of. Here are two you can make at home, Rose of Warsaw and Polish Flag Shot.*

PRASKIE KOKTAJLE

# *Praga Cocktails*

## WARSZAWSKA RÓŻA *Rose of Warsaw*

FOR 1 DRINK

2 parts vodka
1 part cherry/raspberry liqueur

Shake the ingredients in a Boston-style shaker two thirds filled with ice.

Strain and serve chilled.

## POLSKA FLAGA *Polish Flag Shot*

FOR 1 DRINK

1 part Cointreau
1 part Grenadine
1 part vodka

Mix the Cointreau with the Grenadine and pour into a glass.

Carefully layer on the vodka by holding an inverted teaspoon as close to the surface of the drink as you can and gently pouring over the vodka. This should create two separate layers.

Sto lat! (100 years!)

*This is an old recipe for Polish honey liqueur. It uses Polish spiritus, a form of pure, rectified alcohol. Served warm, it will put festive spirit into the grumpiest Christmas guest.*

KRUPNIK POLSKI

# Honey-spiced Liqueur

120 ml (½ cup) spiritus (or 240 ml (1 cup) vodka)
120 ml (½ cup) honey
0.5 l (2 cups) water
1 teaspoon ground cloves
8 whole peppercorns
1 stick cinnamon
1 teaspoon nutmeg
1 teaspoon ground ginger
1 teaspoon ground all spice
zest of ½ orange
½ vanilla pod (split)

Put the water, cloves, peppercorns, cinnamon, nutmeg, ginger, all spice, orange zest and vanilla pod in a saucepan. Bring to the boil and simmer gently, covered, for 5 minutes.

Strain through a muslin cloth (cheesecloth) or fine tea strainer. Return to the heat and add the honey. Bring to the boil and immediately remove from the heat.

When the drink has cooled slightly, stir in the spiritus or vodka. Serve warm.

POLSKA

POLSKA

# Birds that Stay

*My schoolbooks were filled with szlaczki – a line of drawings to mark the end of homework each day.*

I remember drawing the birds that did not leave Poland for winter. They were red robins, sparrows and yellow tits that regularly visited the wooden table (a school carpentry project) on the window sill outside. Unlike the storks, they did not fly away in winter, and remained my loyal friends.

I stood quietly and watched through the thick glass as the tiny creatures flew in and out pecking at a piece of old bread or the strip of fatty smoked bacon I had smuggled from Mama Druga's kitchen. I hoped the big black crow, also watching the show from a nearby pine, would not swoop again and grab the bacon, spoiling my bird theatre.

BELOW A szlaczek by Misia Bajor, aged 6. The decorative pattern to mark the end of homework reads: "The birds that don't fly away to warm countries in winter".

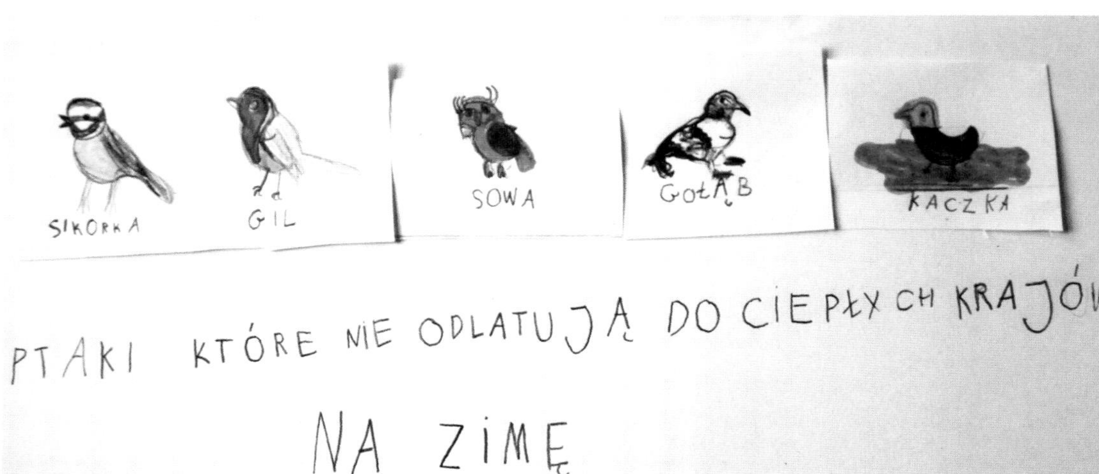

# Flying Away

It is the end of January and our winter trip is over. Returning to Australia I know I must put away my childhood memories.

As the plane climbs above the airport I can see a red neon light spelling out "Warszawa". The name gets smaller and smaller with every deep sigh. I think about the sad moment of undressing the Christmas tree with my grandmother Józefa. I had to put back all the glass decorations into boxes, cover them with lots of hay and newspaper, and replace them in the attic behind a curtain of great grandmother Julia's poppy-seed husks, garlands of garlic, and dried mushrooms. They would make their return appearance another December but, until then, they had to dream alone of the next Christmas Eve.

My head pressed against the cold plane window, I can clearly see Julia and Józefa standing under the snow-covered linden tree, waving goodbye. Calm and smiling, they know they are immortal to me, and their love coats me with a shiny armour, like the sugar coating on bitter orange peel. Months or years may fly by again, but I shall return to Poland, with those faithless storks, just as soon as the snow melts.

# *from 'Poems'*

In the windows this land rushes by, the trees, the fields run.
The snow glitters on branches, slides off in the sun.
It is green again: young green at first, then ripe, then
green extinguished like candles.
Poland: the land rushes by, in green, in autumn, in snow.
A traveler on foot takes it in - it's a long way
to walk from end to end.
A bird can scarcely cross the land, only a plane
absorbs this space in an hour, squaring the native land
with its wings.

by Karol Wojtyła, Pope John Paul II, 1979
trans. Jerzy Peterkiewicz

*Ziemia przebiega w oknach, przebiegają drzewa i pola.*
*I mieni się śnieg na gałęziach, a potem w słońcu opada.*
*I znowu zieleń: młoda naprzód, potem dojrzała, wreszcie gasnąca jak świece.*

*Ziemia polska przebiega w zieleniach, jesieniach i śniegach,*
*Chłonie ją pieszy wędrowiec — z krańca do krańca trudno przejść.*
*I ptak nie przeleci tak łatwo, lecz samolot*
*w godzinę pochłonie tę przestrzeń — Ojczyznę zamknie w swój kwadrat.*

BALTIC SEA
LITHUANIA
BELARUS
UKRAINE
SLOVAKIA
CZECH REPUBLIC
GERMANY
A winter tour of
POLAND
Kołobrzeg
Ryn
Giżycko
Mazury Lakes
Tykocin
Białystok
Białowieża
WARSZAWA
Wolsztyn
Łódź
Lublin
Jelenia Góra
Karpacz
Książ
Karkonosze Mountains
Kraków
Tarnów
Łańcut
Wieliczka
Tatra Mountains
Zakopane
N
S
E
W

# Lista Przepisów  List of Recipes

# Index

Numbers in *italics* refer to illustrations.

OPPOSITE 'Grandmother's name day' by Olga Boznańska, 1889

# Acknowledgements

The authors would like to thank the following individuals and institutions for their kind permission to reproduce material in this book:

Silesian Museum, Katowice
Stanisław Kamocki (1875-1944): 'Winter' [p.6]
Olga Boznańska (1865-1940) 'Two Girls' [p.133]

National Museum, Wrocław
Władysław Ślewiński (1854-1918): 'Roses and chamomile' [p.9]

Marcel Weyland
Translation of extracts from:
Juliusz Słowacki (1809-1849): 'Lines in Zofia's Autograph Album' [p.10]
Władysław Broniewski (1897-1962) 'To the Jews of Poland' [p.255]
Adam Mickiewicz (1798-1855): Epilogue 'Land of Childhood' from Pan Tadeusz [p. 170]
Above extracts originally published in 'The Word - Two Hundred Years of Polish Poetry' Brandl & Schlesinger (2010) and 'Pan Tadeusz' Verand Press (2004)

National Museum, Poznań
Józef Pankiewicz (1866-1940): 'Warsaw Old Town Square at Night' [p.45]
Kazimierz Wojniakowski (1771-1812): 'Hope' [p.141]
Teodor Axentowicz (1859-1938): 'Portrait of a Woman in a Black Dress' [p.183]
Stanisław Wyspiański (1869-1907) 'Staś sleeping' [p. 155]

National Museum, Kraków
Władysław Podkowiński, View of Nowy Świat, Warsaw in winter [p.47]

Wilanów Palace Museum
Marcello Bacciarelli (1731-1818): Portrait of Izabela Lubomirska, phot. Zbigniew Reszka [p.65]

Płock Mazowian Museum
Stanisław Wyspiański (1869-1907) 'A Country Madonna' [p. 160]

National Museum, Warsaw
Tadeusz Makowski (1882-1932): 'Children with a turoń (monster)' [p.171]
Olga Boznańska (1865-1940): 'Grandmother's name day' [p.311]

Leszek & Alina Mądzik
Fine Art Gallery, Catholic University, Lublin (KUL)
The Madonna and Baby, 16th-century fresco [p.71]

Elisabeth & Ulrich von Küster, Łomnica Palace private collection, G. Mattis, 'Waterfall' [p.178]

Ela Chylewska, Christmas Carol, trans. Natalia O'Keefe [p.117]

Museum of Fashion and Textiles ITE, Białystok
1960s Polish dress patterns [p.191]

Walter Whipple
tranlastion of 'The Locomotive' by Julian Tuwim (1894-1953) [p.227]

Adam Bartosz

'Catalogue of the Romany Collections at the Museum of Tarnów' I. Tarczałowicz'Cyganka' 1889 [p.269]

Libreria Editrice Vaticana extract from 'Poems' by Karol Wojtyła (Pope John Paul II) (1920-2005) trans. Jerzy Peterkiewicz
Weronika Litwin
Preservation of Jewish Heritage in Poland

Jolanta Ścibior
Museum of Lublin

Rafał Stachurski
Wieliczka Salt Mine

Katarzyna Matuła
Książ Castle

Special thanks to:
Lidia & Grzegorz Zatorski, Jan & Sabina Bajor, Maciej & Małgosia Bajor, Jane Aspden, Nick Barry, Adam Bartosz, Beata Bieniek, Katarzyna Cegłowska, Ela Chylewska, Henryk and Joanna Dumin, Daniel Gromann, Yaja Hadrys, Miranda Harvey, Krzysztof Izdebski, Andrzej & Nuna Jaroszyński, Kazimiera Karpuk, Elizabeth Kopff, Elisabeth von Küster, Leszek & Alina Mądzik, Pola Sobaś-Mikołajczyk, Michael Moran, Anna & Jim Parton, Konrad Pyzel, Veronica Sumegi, George Target, Julian Target, Tomasz Wagner, Connie and Jonathan Webber, Wit Karol Wojtowicz, Wiesława Wilczyńska, Iga Zatorska.

Gertie Jaquet gertiejacquet.blogspot.nl
Eliza Mórawska www.whiteplate.blogspot.com
Barbara Rolek www.easteuropeanfood.about.com

Map of Poland on page 305 by George Target

Additional photograpy: Maciej Bajor 1,2,9,16.17, 25, 46,85,86, 121, 123, 142, 176, 179, 186, 230, 231, 261, 298, 302 Iga Zatorska 48,59 Katarzyna Cegłowska 87, 158, 170, 209, 211, 262 Tomasz Wagner 49 Jim Parton 96 Yaja Hadrys 106 Leena Klockars 145

SUGARED ORANGE

by Beata Zatorska and Simon Target
First published in 2013 by Tabula Books, London and Sydney

www.tabulabooks.com



British Cataloguing-in-Publication Data

A catalogue record for this book is available from the British Library

ISBN 978-0-956699-22-0

Photography: Simon Target

Design and Editing: Tabula

Design final review: Kerry Klinner

Prepress: Graphic Print Group

Printed and bound in China by 1010 Printing International Ltd

Typeset in Dear Sarah and Mrs Eaves

To order please contact
www.tabulabooks.com